PET GREYHOUNDS in TOWNS & CITIES

Mary Fox

cover photo by Eimhin McNamara
images by Jessica Reid

Copyright © 2016 Mary Fox
All rights reserved.
ISBN: **1535145927**
ISBN-13: **978-1535145923**

CONTENTS

	Preface	i
1	Greyhounds in the 21st Century	1
2	Houses & Apartments	11
3	Basic Needs Out Walking	24
4	Basic Needs at Home	37
5	Basic Training or Rules of the Road	57
6	Out and About in Public Spaces	70
7	Problems in Public Space & First Aid	85
8	Off-leash Freedom & the Runaway Greyhound	99
9	Whether the Weather…	109
10	A Few Final Words	116
	Appendix	118

Dedicated to Jeanette Woods, who was on the ground floor of promoting ex-racing greyhounds as pets many years ago, and to Maggie Greyhound, who defied the odds and found love.

Mary Fox

Preface

The idea for this second book on greyhounds as pets arose when several important issues surfaced within a few months of each other. The first was that more and more people globally were adopting greyhounds, other sighthounds, and crosses of those dogs, and that many of these adopters were living in urban areas. The slow global collapse of the racing industry alerts us all to a growing and continuing need for more responsible homes for tens of thousands of unwanted greyhounds...and most of these homes are likely to be in urban areas. However, there is an information gap on the particular challenges of having a greyhound "in town".

This information gap has become clear in recent times. Contrary to the relaxed and gentle nature of our long nosed, deep-chested, whip-tailed, leggy companions, many new adopters often have little to no guidance from their adoption groups, who themselves are often new to greyhounds and similar dogs. From not being told about the necessity of things like martingale collars and specific anaesthetic needs to off leash realities and feeding suggestions, adopters sometimes are left dangling to figure things out for themselves. Living with any type of sighthound in a town or city can present some challenges anyway, and this book aims to address those challenges.

This book is based partly on conversations I have had with people from different urban areas. Of particular inspiration was a closed Dublin-based FaceBook group. Here, individuals from among close to 600 members would post daily, seeking advice on a range of issues, looking for walking partners, and just celebrating life with their hounds. The group's founder watched it quickly become a meeting point and resource for sighthound owners.

Part of this book is also based on what I learned from over 10 years' experience running a greyhound sanctuary on my own. Orchard Greyhound Sanctuary had up to 18 dogs at a time, where they lived in carefully selected small groups instead of individual kennels. I put 24/7 into it and got to know the hounds very well. For health reasons I dramatically downsized, and some of my learned experience as well as historical reading became part of my first book on pet greyhounds, ***Understanding Greyhounds: Our Companions Through the Ages.*** There is a smidge of overlap between that book and this one, both in text and some images, but it is minimal. Where

Understanding Greyhounds is much more in-depth on all issues, this book specifically addresses the urban greyhound

Two more comments: first, I am not a certified canine trainer or behaviourist, and so am not promoting the latest theory...which is soon to be eclipsed by another theory. Sighthounds need to be approached differently on some matters – such as recall – and the idea that all dogs are absolutely the same when it comes to training is overly simplistic. And second, in the interest of canine gender equality, in this book I always use female terms instead of the more common male assumption.

Now to thank those who gave encouragement, ideas, or assistance: Gary Brady, Maureen Byrne, Jane Castel, Nathalie Cloux, Jilly Cooper, Sarah Crinion, Sharon Darby, James Dennis, Carole Devaney, Bob Edwards, Marie Heuzé, Cat Hughes, Annette Hunter, Una Jansen, Mary Kennedy, Kate Lee, Tracey Long, Orla McCluskey, Pat O'Hare, Lisa Martinez, Ken and Noelle Pace *(yes that's how I think of you two!)*, Dawn Priory, Jessica Reid, Jack Rourk, Pete Wedderburn, and the indefatigable Wendy Willson. Great thanks to the various rescues who routinely promote my previous book to their adopters, especially to Homes for Unwanted Greyhounds (HUG), who give it away to new adopters.

Special thanks to the cover's model Haizea, her owner Aitziber Barona, and that prince of a fellow Eimhin McNamara, who came through with several great cover photo shots at the 11th hour! I must thank my own long-suffering hounds who put up with insane sleeping and rising hours and long periods of waiting for me to leave the computer for a walkaround break. Tim the lurcher, Molly the elderly greyhound, recently deceased, magnificent gentle Arrian, and Henry, the tallest wuss of a greyhound there is, thank you for being such patient hounds and good company!

Mary Fox
Ireland
SEPTEMBER 2016

1 GREYHOUNDS IN THE 21ST CENTURY

"There is reason to believe that as long as 12,000 years ago humans chose to domesticate, rather than hunt, the dog. The primary evidence...was uncovered in the remains of a stone dwelling...in northern Israel...Found there was a human skeleton, flexed on its right side, with its hand upon what the researchers have determined to be the remains of a three- to five-month-old puppy."[1]

The most important starting point for this book is that we humans have been with dogs for thousands of years. The archaeological record shows that for close to half of that, some of those dogs have been some type of sighthound. This book is not only for greyhounds, but for similar dogs as well, though the word *greyhound* will be used throughout. There are so many dogs who are part greyhound, or are another sighthound breed all together, and much of what is written here can also apply to many of them. Of course, some of what is in these pages can apply to many types and breeds of dogs, but there are issues which mainly apply to greyhounds and their near relatives. That said, this book is specifically written for long-legged, pointy-nosed, deep-chested, small-waisted dogs of sighthound and particularly greyhound background. This includes Whippets, Salukis, Sloughis, Deerhounds, Wolfhounds and more, as well as their crosses.

Having a pet greyhound in your life in the twenty-first century and living in any sort of built-up environment has its own special advantages and challenges. The advantage is that most greyhounds are undemanding and quiet, and in spite of their size, having such greyhounds makes life

---

[1] "Early Dog: Cro-Magnon's Best Friend", *Science News*, Vol. 114, No. 26 (Dec. 23-30, 1978), p. 438.

surprisingly easy, far easier than most people can believe. Their ability to quietly curl up under a table or in their dog bed or, ok, I admit it, to sprawl out glamorously across a bed or sofa, and to stay there quietly for hours at a time is well known among their owners. Many will claim their greyhounds sleep about 22 hours a day, and that would not be an exaggeration for most greyhounds, even young ones. If you are looking for a busy dog who is always underfoot and always up to something, then don't get a greyhound!

Their generally largish size[2] combined with their generally quiet nature makes them big enough to be intimidating to burglars, but quiet enough to be appreciated by the neighbour who might have barky terriers or collies or a German Shepherd living on the other side of them. Fundamentally, there is no down side to a greyhound living in an urban environment per se, and most obstacles are able to be addressed. However, we have to keep in mind that an urban environment is not natural to them, and living in towns, cities, or city suburbs in this day and age puts up enormous challenges to any greyhound and greyhound owner. Besides having to deal with constant, fast-paced and often frightening traffic as well as possible problems with close neighbours, there is also discarded food and broken glass on the ground, lack of open spaces, dog parks, friendly and unfriendly loose dogs, cats hiding under cars, screaming children, apartment living, and more. This book intends to address them one step at a time.

To address these issues in a practical and meaningful way requires a thorough response, and so this book is a follow-on from my first work on this subject, **Understanding Greyhounds: Our Companions Through the Ages**. The issues more thoroughly covered in this first book involve: greyhound and sighthound history and why it is important today; selecting a greyhound; your first hours, days and weeks with your new companion; training and bonding; practical needs; behaviour problems; greyhounds and small animals; greyhounds and children; a separate chapter on recall; and finally health and first aid. However, coping with the contemporary world is far too broad of a topic to have included in the first book, and really deserved to be fleshed out as much as possible and not squeezed into one chapter. So no matter if you already have a greyhound who needs to adapt better to urban life or you are thinking about getting yourself a greyhound

---

[2] Some greyhounds can be relatively tiny from 23 inches/59cm at the top of the back, while others can be quite large, to about 31 inches/79cm at the top of the back. However, most greyhounds range between 25-28 inches/63-71cm at the top of the back.

companion, this book is meant to give you some realistic, hands-on tips and ideas on dealing with some of the problems that modern life puts in front of us. Greyhounds have their own special set of considerations that are well worth being aware of, and which will make your shared lives much easier if you take a little time to understand them.

Developing a relationship with your greyhound is the first order of business, and from there you can work on being able to teach a few very basic cues and manners which serve as a foundation upon which the rest of your lives together will be built. Many of us who have or want pet greyhounds have a lovely image in our minds that we see other people doing, and we want it too: it's a sunny day, not too hot, and not too cold, and we are walking our beautiful greyhound down the street. Everything is fine and nothing rattles our Prince or Princess Among Dogs, not a bit. They walk close to us on a loose leash, exuding a quiet calm and a certain self-confidence, and they stay that way throughout the walk. Large trucks roar past us, ambulances scream by, and our greyhound is unflappable. People pass us with their shrill-throated tiny dogs and they are envious, as are other people being dragged by their uncontrollable large dogs. We might even let ourselves inside the dog park, unclipping our dog's leash, and smiling to ourselves as she never wanders more than a few meters from our sides, and other owners stare resentfully. We laugh. We have the best dog ever, and people marvel at our Perfect Urban Greyhound.

It just looks so easy.

Well, for some greyhounds it IS easy, but for others, they might need to work at it a bit to learn that it's easy. Of course, while some of us are dreaming about the perfect day and perfect greyhound, others would be happy if our dog would just please stop trying to eat their child's ice cream or lunging at every dog that is not at least knee-high. It might be good to keep our expectations reasonable as we aim towards turning our greyhound into managing various demands and distractions. Some greyhounds might be well able to take on a lot at once, and others need to proceed step by step. With this is mind, perhaps one of the most helpful things you can do for yourself is to determine if your dog or the one you are hoping to adopt might be amenable to city life. I should say that by "city", I mean urban living: everything from inner city living to life at the edge of town to perhaps having to visit urban areas with your dog frequently.

Greyhounds and urban life
The good news is that, in general, ex-racing greyhounds often easily adapt to city living. This is because if they had been raced often, they were exposed to a range of sensory stimulants already at the racetrack. Think about what being at the racetrack meant: the buzz of excitement in the air, traffic in the car park, being moved in and out of a vehicle, large groups of people, cheering in the stands and constant movement, people they did not know handling them, bright lights, the smell of food, the sight of other dogs behind the scenes and not interacting with them, the loudspeaker system, even racing alongside other dogs and not interfering with them and then being caught and leashed up after the race…all these experiences can be useful skills for a pet adapting to built-up areas. From ear-piercing sirens to strangers wanting to pet them, not always interacting with other dogs and having to stay on the leash – in this way, life as a pet in the city is not SO very different from being a racing dog. In addition, they often have developed nerves of steel, and don't go flying in another direction at the first sign of something unusual. So an ex-racing greyhound is often well-prepared for such a life. There is a down side, too, and I will get to that.

First, we need to divide this discussion into two parts, as there is a big difference between _selecting_ a dog likely to be good out in busy public areas versus _training or conditioning a greyhound you already have_ for that lifestyle. The second part is if you already have a greyhound, and want to improve on your greyhound's strengths and weaknesses while manoeuvring her through city life *(yes, as mentioned in the preface, I do refer to your greyhound as **her** throughout this book, to introduce some gender balance for all the books that refer to your greyhound as **him**!)*. In terms of weaknesses, for example, some people, no matter if their greyhound is recently adopted or not, might complain that their greyhound is always a problem in certain circumstances in urban areas. A more careful observation of those circumstances and a bit of a shift in thinking might go a long way in helping the greyhound – and the owner – to cope better.

It's important that you are clear in your own mind if you really want to have a greyhound in your constant care or maybe you would be best off by taking this a step at a time to find out. Just for starters, you might begin to get a better feel for this by helping out an adoption centre that welcomes volunteers to help with caring for and walking their greyhounds. Here, you can get to know greyhounds a little better. You might deliberately choose a centre that is at the edge of a town and deliberately walks the dogs through it on occasion. From there, you might go the next step and foster one of their greyhounds at home until it is adopted. The point here is that if you already live in a busy area and are not certain you want to make the commitment of owning a greyhound while living in the city, you don't have to make a big leap. Instead, you can go a step at a time and see what it's like in stages.

Selecting the right greyhound
The first point to make here is that even though you might be living in a small terraced house or an apartment, choosing to adopt a greyhound over other, smaller dogs is something you might be criticized for. Considering the greyhound size range, however, some criticism might be coming from people who have only seen very large greyhounds. But more importantly, no matter how tall they are, greyhounds often have a lovely capacity to make themselves very small and very still most of the time, and are not the sort of dog that is always underfoot and always "on the job", seeking your attention, needing something to do. So physically big – sometimes, yes. But most of the time, they are a quiet and unobtrusive presence in the home. More about this in Chapter 2 on terraced house and apartment life.

If you are seeking a greyhound to adopt and don't have a lot of experience training a dog, then you know you need a greyhound who from the start is likely to be good in a high-traffic or congested area. This applies no matter if you actually live in the centre of the city, or bring your dog into the city with you daily, or simply visit there frequently enough where you need a dog who already has some basic possible fears out of the way. We can think of being able to handle traffic as a desirable "non-issue" – you want a greyhound where standing at a traffic light at a busy intersection, with cars and trucks flying by and people congregating is a non-issue. In such a case, an experienced racing dog is a good candidate. No matter if you are considering a greyhound from a rescue and rehoming group or directly from an owner or trainer, an experienced racer is a good place to start because it is not an absolute guarantee, but can be promising. For your first greyhound, however, you probably are better off adopting straight from a rescue, who should be able to give you some general guidance.[3]

Most racing greyhounds stop racing at about four or five years old. Many greyhounds live to be twelve or more, so adopting a four or five year old greyhound is not adopting an old dog. In fact, it's a great age and a great time to adopt them. Besides it being an age where most dogs will begin to settle down and not have too much youthful exuberance, most are very happy to retire, and they settle into home life very quickly. Some might have some old injuries that are just beginning to hinder them, and this makes them unsuitable for the demands of further racing, but perfect for the demands of being a pet. It would not be unusual for a vet to examine an old injury and recommend that the injury is not treatable, and the dog should only get light exercise, such as leashed walks and limited time running off leash. Sounds perfect.

What can be very revealing, if possible, is to find out your greyhound's racing history. This can tell you a lot. How you find out the history can vary – it is best is if there is an online database that you can return to if need be. Some of them list greyhounds according to their racing name, others according to their ear tattoos, and some will do both. Online databases are very handy because usually you can see the following information besides date of birth, breeder and pedigree: how frequently the dog was raced; how many different tracks the dog raced at; if the dog tended to race at very well-known tracks with high attendance or more rural and less frequented tracks. These points will all give you an idea of your greyhound's capacity for an urban lifestyle. Some databases might also indicate if your greyhound was disqualified for fighting.

---

[3] For a fuller discussion on selecting a greyhound, including where to look, see the relevant chapters in my previous book, **Understanding Greyhounds: Our Companions Through the Ages (2015)**; available on Amazon.

To use two extremes to illustrate a point: you might be encouraged to adopt a greyhound who you are told "oh yes, she was raced all right…" However, looking into the greyhound's background you find that she only raced three times, and it was at a rural or low-attendance track. This does not rule her out immediately, but should signal to you to proceed with caution, as she might not have continued racing because she could not perform under the stress of the track. Most owners and trainers would not admit to something like this as a reason for not continuing racing her, but would just say "she couldn't run" or something similar. They generally don't think in terms of a greyhound's mental state. "Can it run?" is their greatest concern. This does not mean that a greyhound who only ran a few times is guaranteed not to be a good candidate, *but it does mean that there is a certain amount you cannot take for granted.*

In contrast, suppose you found out there was an error, and the greyhound in fact ran 30 races, not 3. This alone could tell you worlds about the dog's confidence level, experience, exposure and more. It would mean that there were 30 times that greyhound was loaded into a vehicle, driven to a noisy, stimulating, distracting, congested greyhound stadium, unloaded from the car or perhaps one of those dreadful greyhound trailers, walked through a busy car park, and then exposed to the sights, sounds and smells and overall buzz of the greyhound track. This is a dog who is almost ready to go home with you – I say almost because there is still a bit of other training involved, BUT the potential problems with daily exposure to congested living is not an issue. In other words, there is enough of a demand and lifestyle change on a new greyhound and its new owner without the added complications of fear of traffic and noise.

Of course, regarding the greyhound with limited track exposure, you can find a way to try the dog out around traffic if the rehoming group or the owner/trainer will allow you, even if they insist on accompanying you. If you are given this chance, there are a few things to consider while trying her out. First, make sure the collar and leash or the harness is correctly fitted and unlikely to be slipped out of, and that the leash is about 6ft/ 180cm long. Leash length is important because while you are walking the greyhound in a relatively quiet place, you can practice letting her have most of the length of the leash, and when you are approaching traffic, a busy road, or a red light, then practice shortening up the leash and making the greyhound walk closer to you. In other words, see how well behaved she is while on the leash, how attentive she is to leash length and stopping to wait, and to slowing down or speeding up with you. These are reasonable expectations and are part of the skills needed to be out walking in the city.

Country greyhound to city greyhound
Of course, there is also the scenario that you might be moving to a more built-up area, or have reason to be visiting one with frequency with your greyhound, and know that your current pet greyhound has had very little exposure to traffic. You can start by building up your greyhound's exposure to the noise and traffic of an urban setting from your quieter home environment. You don't necessarily have to begin by traveling to the place you will be moving to for a series of visits. If it is too far away for visits, then simply begin by working a bit within your current home environment or a small town closer to you.

Even beginning in small and gradual ways is possible. Perhaps you can start taking walks when the local school bus is picking up or dropping off children: you can stand very close to where it passes by or even closer when it is leaving a student off the bus. If a delivery or service vehicle comes to your house, go outside with your greyhound to greet the driver. If there is a small town nearby, start bringing your greyhound there on a regular basis. All in all, no matter if you are exposing your greyhound to nearby environments or are able to go directly to the "target" environment and practice from there, it's best to start doing so at very slow periods during daylight hours, such as early Sunday mornings or a weeknight evening.

As you increasingly expose your greyhound to more challenges, keep in mind this is a time when her confidence level in both yourself and herself should begin to grow if you are not overfacing her. Taking her to the same places and gradually changing the time of day to busier and busier hours is a good way to start. By doing this, with let's say the first three visits during very quiet times, then when you begin to change the visits to the busier times, your greyhound will already be familiar with the area, will know what to expect, and so slight increases in traffic and general activity will not be too big of a shock to her system. Although this might seem a bit tedious or long and drawn out, _it always pays off in the long run to make progress in steps or stages._ Your greyhound gradually introduced to traffic and the city in ten visits instead of five visits will make a sounder and more well adjusted dog. It can be a good habit, when possible, to walk your greyhound through the less demanding or easy spots at the beginning of a walk, then to the more demanding places at the end of the walk when the edge is off of her. ***This work you do in the beginning is the foundation upon which the rest of her time in a busy environment will be based. You only have one chance to make a good first impression, so do it with patience, reward (irresistible treats and stroking) and a lot of repetition. If you rush it too much, then you will have to start all over again.***

Remember that the more you work with your greyhound in the beginning, the more you are also conditioning her to leashed exercise. Make sure on your walks you do go somewhere that she can really enjoy…..after all, trudging down a concrete pavement has its limits for any dog in terms of being interesting. At some point during the walk she should have access to a grassy area or a beach or some spot where, even if you can't let her off the leash, at least you can long-leash her. By making sure she always gets exposed to somewhere interesting, then she always has something to look forward to, knowing she will at least enjoy some long-leashing in the process. Long-leashing is discussed more fully in later chapters.

In regard to bringing your greyhound with you when driving into any town, just regularly being exposed to the sights and sounds of other cars, traffic in general, and other people from the safety of her "own car" is a help. The more you take her out in the beginning, the better she becomes on the leash in general….and since some greyhounds have some real size to them and can be strong, then the better she is on the leash, the more easy it will be for you have control. In a busy, noisy, unpredictable environment, if your greyhound gets frightened, you need to be well able to control her. The skills and bond you will have been developing over time will have a major part to play in your greyhound's adjustment. Perhaps you might think about furthering the bond with your greyhound. This is fine, of course, as long as it does not *always* involve food, since food is not going to be the main driver of the trust your "city greyhound" will have in you. The _bonding = food_ equation is incorrect. Of course, bonding can sometimes be practiced through food, but it can also be practiced through belly rubs, body rubs, and a reassuring hand that says you are protector and guide, too.

Your greyhound will look to you for guidance in challenging or intimidating situations, even when _you also_ might feel challenged or intimidated. In such situations, you will need to take hold of the problem and be decisive and not panic. No matter if you have adopted a greyhound who seems well used to traffic, or is one you are exposing and conditioning to traffic, now and then she might experience a genuine fright and won't want to go out any more. In fact, _you_ might not want to go out any more either, but here you will need to take hold: _**if you** don't, no one else will_. You can begin at the beginning, going so slowly that your greyhound will become impatient and begin to accelerate the process on her own, and bring you along too. This is a good sign, meaning she is feeling confident again, and you can too.

Greyhounds adjusting to city life is a far cry from thousands of years of a very different type of life they had been living. Some traits that carried them through time and in rural environments are ironically the same traits that we can adapt to today. However, it is a mistake to see it as irony; almost 2000 years ago the Greek historian Arrian crowed about his own greyhound, Hormé, whom he mentioned in his famous book about greyhounds (*vertraha*) **On Coursing** (*Cynegeticus*). Our greyhounds were city dogs even then, Rome and Athens being very busy, noisy, full of distractions and needing to be negotiated wisely for off-leash hounds. Arrian tells us:

> *But while I am at home, he remains within, by my side, accompanies me on going abroad, follows me to the gymnasium, and, while I am taking exercise, sits down by me. On my return, he runs before me, often looking back to see whether I had turned any where out of the road; and as soon as he catches sight of me, showing symptoms of joy, and again trotting on before me.* [4]

A pair of sighthounds from Arrian's time, about 0-100AD

---

[4] Arrian, *Cynegeticus* (London: J. Bohn, 1831), 79-81

2 HOUSES AND APARTMENTS

"My Gonzo is a perfect example of a greyhound adapting to apartment life. He really has turned into a go-anywhere, do-anything kind of dog. I can literally walk him and take him anywhere, he's bomb-proof with all kinds of traffic, loves meeting people and other dogs, and some local shops welcome both of us when I am out walking. Best of all, a local café happily allows Gonzo in, where he finds himself a nice cushy spot on the sofa at the back of the café." (Gary B, Dublin, Gonzo's best friend and avid café-goer; see Gonzo below!)

No matter if you have a detached or semi-detached house with a small garden, or a second floor apartment, some of the commitments and challenges of having a greyhound in any kind of a built-up area are the same. There are some important differences, and these are dealt with separately and later in this chapter. When people who live in urban areas read about how greyhounds can be couch potatoes, how relaxed and undemanding they can be, and how many of them are generally quiet, then adopting a greyhound sounds like a good idea. And it can be.

Of course some people might advise potential greyhound owners that it would be wiser to look for a smaller dog, a nice little terrier, perhaps, or a spaniel of some sort.

However, they would be unaware how quiet and settled most greyhounds can be, and overlooking the reality that most terriers and spaniels are likely to be more underfoot, more present, more demanding and more barky than most greyhounds. Greyhounds don't generally follow you around and say *"what are you doing?.......and what are you doing now?........and NOW what are you doing? Can you pet me? Can you pet me again? Are we going out soon? Are we going out NOW please? Do you have a treat for me?"* and so on.

Most greyhounds are very happy indeed to go for a morning walk, snooze on the sofa or their bed for awhile, get up, eat, drink some water, and then return to sleep. And they assume all sorts of contorted positions when doing so. They don't want to be underfoot, they don't want to bark at every little noise, and they are happy to see the leash but won't be begging you for it. So yes, greyhounds in general can be very well disposed to town or city life. Within the home they tend to fold themselves up, so to speak, and some visitors might even comment they had no idea a dog was in the house. In fact, as I write, 4 greyhounds and 1 lurcher are curled up on beds in my kitchen. It is a rainy day. The back door is open so they can go out if they want, but they are happy to be inside and away from the rain. No one is

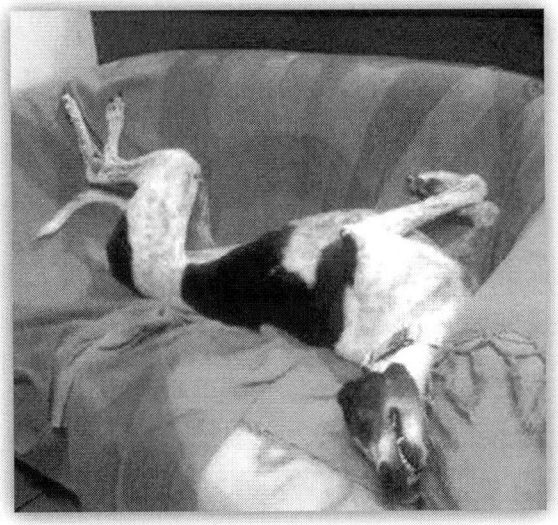

barking or crying for attention, electrical cords are not being chewed, the furniture is safe and no one is surfing the kitchen worktop. Greyhounds are generally quiet souls.

There are a few things your urban greyhound needs to grasp or have for happily living in a house or apartment in a built-up area:

- toileting
- reacting to outside stimuli
- body awareness
- visitors

- noise (from your greyhound)
- adequate sleeping/resting areas
- socializing with other dogs

Let's take these one at a time:

Toileting

Life is going to be a problem for both of you if this is not well established right away. Perhaps the two most important keys to success in this area are establishing a routine and getting to know your greyhound's habits. Put another way, coordinating feeding times with your preferred times for toileting breaks can take a bit of thinking through, but will be well worth it in the long run. You will need to watch for how long it takes for food to pass through your greyhound's digestive system, as it can vary between individuals and according to what they have eaten. If you greyhound needs only about 4 hours, then feeding at 7pm, for example, and having the "last call" at 10pm might be unwise.

If you have a garden, some greyhounds might refuse to perform unless you are outside with them, or if it is cold or raining. Going outside with your greyhound does run the risk of you being a distraction and her just standing next to you and begging to go back in. For a number of reasons, it is better for you and her that she learn to perform on her own. A week or two of you being resolute about this is necessary. If you feed at 6 and your greyhound is reluctant to go out at 10:30, for example, put her out anyway, and DON'T stand at the door watching. Instead, turn on an outside light and step back. During these early days you should watch, but do so without your greyhound being able to see you, and most important of all, **_time it_**. Be ready to wait twenty minutes. _The very moment_ your greyhound has performed, immediately open the door and welcome her back in. A few nights of this and she will understand quickly what is wanted of her. If you are consistent, it will get to the point where she will rush outside in any weather, immediately do what she is supposed to do, and rush right back in. When your greyhound gets to this point, you will feel like one of the luckiest people in the world.

Reacting to outside stimuli

No matter if you are living on a narrow back street or a main thoroughfare, your greyhound is going to be aware of the sights, sounds and smells of what is "out there" and not coming from within the house. You might do well to put yourself in your greyhound's mind and understand what it is like for her, in the house, hearing something interesting or exciting outside, and not being able to investigate.

You then might want to give your greyhound access to a window where she can look outside and watch the world going by. It would have to be a window which is at her eye level, OR which she can see from when she is perched on a chair or sofa, OR a window she can stand up on her back legs to look out. It does not necessarily have to be a front window: the owner of one city-living lurcher was very concerned that his girl spent a lot of time upstairs on his bed, even when he was downstairs watching tv or eating. He actually wondered if she was unhappy and wanted to be away from him. I looked at the room, and it turned out that the bed was a perfect vantage point from which to "oversee" the back garden and the neighbourhood cats who sometimes passed through. To her, being up on the bed was like watching tv. The ideal situation would be a window your greyhound can see from while resting: this encourages a low reaction from her, whereas standing on all fours or on the back legs is a more active position and might encourage over-reaction to outside stimuli.

In terms of very loud noises out on the street that might frighten your greyhound, such as sirens or fireworks, you might think about having a makeshift den or air-raid shelter. By this I mean a small room or even a closet your greyhound can retreat to when frightened. Perhaps you have an older apartment with a pantry that is furthest back from the street, and in which you can place a thick old duvet which will help muffle the noise. Even draping a blanket over a small table and creating a "cave" is another idea…..or just making a small closet floor available, pushing your shoes to the back or sides of it, for example, and throwing some dog bedding on the floor and half closing the door can be very comforting for your greyhound. In the closet, sounds are muffled again by the clothing and boxes in it, and your greyhound is surrounded by the scent of you and does not feel very exposed when you leave that door half closed. These little shelters are places where your greyhound can learn to cope with the noise, and eventually retreat to less and less frequently and for shorter periods of time.

Body awareness

If your home or apartment has small rooms and narrow hallways, life might be a bit easier if your greyhound knows to step aside when need be. Some examples are: when you are coming through the door with 3 heavy bags of groceries; rushing to answer a potentially important phone call; answering the door for an impatient delivery man; or simply moving from one room to the other with a newborn baby in your arms.

Teaching your greyhound to step aside is not just a convenience, but teaches her a body awareness that could be potentially life-saving if she gets loose and sees cars coming her way. Where many dogs will simply ignore a car or stand motionless in its path, a pre-conditioned greyhound is more likely to get out of the way. It could be a useful reflex for her to have in any number of situations.

To convey this, your body language is essential, although it can be handy to include a simple key word. Now don't laugh, but I use **excuse me**, and how I say it depends on the urgency of the situation. It sounds terribly polite! You can begin this too, starting with your greyhound literally standing in your path as you are heading for a chair or the door or anywhere. Normally you might walk around your greyhound, even though your target is directly between you and her. Instead of walking around her, walk right up to her, *make no eye contact*, and guide and push her aside with your knee or calf. At first she might not understand what you are doing, or what you want. Once she begins to catch on, start using a word with it, and even "excuse me" will do. <u>The more consistently you do this, the more quickly she will learn.</u> Eventually, you will not need to use your knee or calf at all, but when she sees you moving towards her, she will begin to automatically step aside, and if she does not, your key word will remind her.

Of course, now and then your greyhound might need reminders, so you might have to "refresh" her sometimes, as needed for any cue or command. With dogs who just don't seem to get it, I might for a day or two pretend I am a particularly heavy footed and clumsy person, letting my feet hit the ground with a thud…your greyhound can feel this through the floor and will automatically step aside. The next time your phone rings and she is between you and the phone, walk towards it with giant steps, lifting your knees high and landing your feet with thud – and watch as she slips out of the way.

Visitors

Perhaps the most important thing your greyhound needs to learn is that not all visitors like dogs. Some will tolerate them, and even those who do like dogs might not want to be accosted, licked, pawed, rubbed against, and so on. I have back problems, for example, and can't stand having someone's large lurcher jump on me, even in happy excitement. However, it's not always convenient or wise to lock a greyhound away for planned or unexpected people in your house, and more important than that, it's not really fair to do it either. Better that your greyhound learns some boundaries with people. From the man who comes in to quickly read your electric meter to the friend who is visiting to cry over a problem, not everyone coming inside wants or should have your greyhound's company, and this is especially so for the painter, floor varnisher or tiler!

Your greyhound would do well to learn self control in increasing amounts. Although you can't expect her to leap from being an over-friendly welcoming committee to willingly retreating to her dog bed in one week, you can begin working on it in small ways. Depending on who is visiting you, you might leash her and sit or stand talking to the person, keeping your greyhound near you and beginning to use a hand signal or key word or both that means "no, you are staying here close to me and not bothering that person". Simply showing your greyhound your palm and pushing your palm _towards_ her face (not IN her face!) is a body language almost all dogs will immediately understand. This is a good start, and it can slowly blossom into your greyhound sometimes even looking to or at you when people arrive, waiting for your cue that tells her what the boundaries are.

Teaching your greyhound _a few key words_ that indicate you want her to go lie down or leave the room, or even to just step back (i.e. _excuse me!_) will benefit you in a range of ways over the years. There are so many ways you can teach these basics, they can't all be covered here. I always taught "go lie down" or "go to bed" from the day a new dog would arrive: for the first few weeks, every time I saw the new dog beginning to lie down, I would say "go to bed" in a monotone voice. The new dog – along with the established dogs – would associate that monotone cue with the act of lying down, and it did not take much for the new hounds to make the connection. In a similar way, every time I let the dogs outside, I would simply say "ok, everybody **OUT**SIDE! **OUT** you go! **OUT** the door." I might even clap my hands or use a sort of waving motion. From here, I could even use it for getting them to vacate certain rooms in the house, for getting off the sofa or out of bed, and more. Yes, I know it's not your standard sausage-waving, highly controlled, training class environment, but it got the job done and made for some very copped-on greyhounds.

Noise levels *(from your greyhound)*
If you live in a town or city, chances are pretty high that you live in close quarters with your neighbours. That said, you need to find ways to be a good neighbour and not let any noise your greyhound might make get out of control. This is not just about barking or howling while you are away or even when you first come home and you are vocally welcomed, but also keeping the noise level down if your greyhound's nails make a lot of noise on a wooden floor, and you have a neighbour directly beneath you.

In regard to howling and barking while you are away, this does not necessarily mean you need to label your greyhound as having "separation anxiety." After all, feeling a bit lonely and expressing it is not separation anxiety, which can be quite severe and particularly destructive. Instead, I am talking about the greyhound who possibly is being left alone too often for too many hours, or is simply not used to being left alone. For the greyhound left alone too much and resorting to barking or howling out of frustration, you need to remedy that with a dog walker, dog day-care, taking the time yourself to get up early and walk your greyhound, or even leaving her with a friend for the day who also has a dog who needs company. Howling or barking out of frustration or boredom does not usually develop from the occasional long day at work, however, and instead usually is the end result of too much of it too often. For those days when you know you might be at work too long, for example, you can leave the radio or tv on, place an unwashed pillowcase or t-shirt (just loaded with your scent) in her dog bed or where ever she tends to rest during the day. You can also get up early and make sure she has an invigorating walk, and when you leave make sure there is something for her to chew on that will take a while. Of course, leaving her with plenty of water and a bit of food is also important.

For the greyhound who is not used to being left alone, you can begin by leaving her alone for short breaks, and slowly increase the amount of time you are away. As the length of the time away increases, then when ever you leave, follow the steps above, handing her the long-term chew just as you are going out the door. By the 4th or 5th time you leave, your greyhound could actually be looking forward to it, because she now KNOWS that your departure is directly connected to something wonderful to eat. Over time you can, if you want, gradually decrease the size of the bone or treat, but in the meantime giving her something like a kong is good because it makes her focus on something else. After working on it for a while, it becomes tiring and the greyhound can often get into the habit of sleeping until you return.

There are other noises which might disturb people living underneath you or sharing a wall with you. Tile or wooden floors accentuate the click-click-click of toenails, for example. You might try keeping your greyhound's nails cut back as much as possible and putting down carpeting in high traffic areas or areas strategic to your neighbour. Even if you love your wooden floors, a few rubber-backed throw rugs can go a long way in not only saving your floors but your neighbour relations too. Since some greyhounds don't like highly smooth surfaces, this is where rubber-backed rugs come in handy.

Sleeping/resting areas
As small as your home might be, there is going to be more than one place where your greyhound likes to rest or sleep. One place might be somewhere that you have assigned, such as a dog bed in your bedroom or perhaps in the kitchen, and the other place often can be of the greyhound's own choosing...and it's usually the sofa. The best location for an extra bed would tend to be places where you and/or other family members can be seen from. For example, if you are often in the kitchen, your greyhound is going to need a bed near enough _that she can see what you are doing and does not feel banished._ Perhaps you spend time in a home office; if so, it would be good to even have just a folded up blanket in there.

Socialising

When living in built-up areas, especially if you live alone, it is easy to become caught up in your own needs and the pattern of your own life, especially to the point where you become very singular. Although many of us are happy to lead that singular life, it is

important to keep in mind that it might not be the so great for your greyhound, who should have some degree of contact with other dogs. If you don't pay attention to this, it is possible for your greyhound to begin to lose her social skills, and become very singular herself. Even if your greyhound just happens to be reserved and self-composed, the occasional company of a suitable dog would be a good idea to arrange. No matter if it's a dog you have met in the park or a friend with a dog who is coming to visit, it is important to make sure the visiting dog's temperament matches or complements your greyhound. An overly wiggly, giddy dog who cannot settle might not be a good choice for a quiet greyhound, for example, though it might not hurt to try, as strange friendships are not impossible. You do need to keep an eye open for when your greyhound has had enough socializing, when she is wanting and needing to retreat to a quiet place. If you don't, then you are inviting a problem.

If you are going to have someone with a dog visit you, be aware of how possessive your greyhound or the visiting dog might be towards any food, treats, or toys that have been left out, or even possessiveness about bedding and people. Asking the visitor about this does not have to be an interrogation, but just a few quick questions so you know what to expect.

One other little tip about visiting dogs is to make sure you always tell visitors with dogs to "make sure" their dog has had a fair chance to toilet before coming in. Even if the owner says the dog had a chance at home anyway, just insist they walk the dog for 5 minutes. It's not worth having new poo or pee in your house, cleaning it up, but always have a scent from the residue present enough for other visiting dogs to pick up on. There is more about cleaning up further down, but the point here is that no matter how well we think we have cleaned it up, even if we can't smell it, **they can**.

Houses with gardens
Having any kind of garden space in towns and cities can at times be hard to come by. There are of course, older homes for sale and rent that might have a tiny front garden and a sizable back garden. For places which have tiny back gardens, there is always the temptation to concrete or tile it over, the idea in mind that it is easier to clean and maintain. However, there are some down sides to this as well. One would be that your greyhound becomes conditioned into assuming that all tile or concrete is ok for toileting, and this can have some frustrating consequences where there is tile or concrete

inside your home, and embarrassing results when you are out visiting. By having a grassy area, it makes them disinclined to toilet anywhere <u>inside</u> that is concrete or tiled, such as the basement, garage, an entryway, the bathroom or kitchen. Getting some dogs to understand that <u>concrete out there is ok but concrete in here is not</u>, can be difficult to convey. This can also be important for when you bring your greyhound on visits to friends or any public places. Unless your greyhound has a very clear understanding in her mind of the difference between inside and outside, this can be difficult to break. In her mind, a cool, smooth surface = ok-to-toilet. And although she might understand it at home eventually, she might not when in other people's homes as well as public places.

If possible, provide your greyhound with a nice grassy area for toileting. You might have an all-concrete/brick/tiles back garden, especially if it's small, but if your greyhound has her own patch of grass at the back of the property, this will have its payoff in the long run. The area should be clearly demarcated from the rest of the patio and could be bordered by bricks, large stones, railroad ties, and be a few inches or cm higher than the rest of the ground around it. You could line it with small stones or gravel, to aid with drainage and then put your soil over it and plant some hardy grass seed. If it measured about 1.5 meters x 1.5 meters (almost 5 ft sq), that should be fine. A slightly larger area, about 3 meters 3 meters, would be even better, since your greyhound might automatically keep one end of it for toileting and the other end for just resting in the sunshine.

Fencing and gates
If you do have a garden of any size and you intend to let your greyhound be in it alone for more than a few minutes, you need fencing. How high? Some people will tell you war stories about greyhounds that could jump a 15 foot/4.5 meter fence, but these kinds of stories need to be taken in stride. The reality is that it all partly depends on the dog, how "trappy" the fencing is, what is along the top of the fence, and how fit, old and settled your greyhound is. If there are a lot of loose cats in your immediate area or urban foxes, this is something to consider, too. Also, in a densely populated area, the fencing is not just for the dog's security but for your own privacy as well, and this could include noise privacy. Stockade fencing can be useful, including some sort of deterrent at the base to keep your greyhound from digging under, though this would be a bit unusual. Sometimes even simple

sheep wire can be cable-tied to existing posts or shrubbery. It all depends on your dog, your neighbours and if they have a dog, and your own preferences.

Gates should be robust, of course, and able to be locked for a number of reasons: your greyhound accidentally getting out is one reason, and a thief too easily getting in is another. You also need to be aware of things like which plants are unsafe for dogs; geraniums, for example, are known to be toxic not only to eat, but even to roll in! One other thing to consider is outside furniture and how you might want to purchase furniture that can withstand a male greyhound who might not notice the difference between lifting his leg on a tree or a table leg.

Apartment Life
Living with a greyhound in an apartment is a little different than living in a terraced house with a small garden. In order to have any dog in an apartment takes a bit of planning, preparedness and strategizing.

The biggest commitment is always being ready and willing and able to take your greyhound outside for toileting no matter what: if you are well or ill, busy or bored, tired or full of energy, have guests or are alone, you have to be ready to take the dog out. The reason why you must avoid any toileting inside is because once it happens. the scent can still be there, discernible to dogs, and it might begin an annoying habit of toileting inside. Even if it happens once, and your greyhound is very sorry about it, this could be picked up by visiting dogs – and thus the cycle continues. So always being prepared to go is a must, and discussed in depth in Chapter 3.

If you do not own a property and have to rely on renting, perhaps the most difficult thing to do in many places is to actually find a landlord who will allow you to have a dog of any kind. In some countries, such as Ireland, there is a broad bias against greyhounds, and as soon as you truthfully answer the question "and what kind of a dog do you have?" you are immediately dismissed. Some landlords have a size range for accepting dogs, and others might want or need reassurance that your dog is not going to eat the woodwork or pull down the shades or blinds. Offering your potential landlord something like a letter from your previous landlord, or a letter of how responsible you are from your vet, or even photos of your dog in the current apartment can often help persuade them that you are not at all like the former tenant whose dog ruined the floors of the apartment or drove the other tenants mad.

Energy Levels
Although the greyhound can and does nicely adjust to urban life, it's good to make sure they do get their fair share of exercise and space or some compensation for it. If you can't let your greyhound off leash for a romp every day, maybe you could invent a doggy game to play, like hide and seek, or finding a toy, or simply rolling a ball or tossing a toy to catch. It does not always have to be the same activity, and you can have different activities on different days. In fact, variation would be particularly stimulating for your greyhound.

One activity a lot of sighthounds enjoy is going to "fun" agility (non-competitive) or flyball sessions. Here they interact with other dogs as well as their owners and are exposed to exciting new ways to play. And don't let anyone tell you "greyhound can't do agility". If someone tells you that, then they have not heard of Never Say Never Greyhounds. This is a remarkable group of greyhounds and their owner defying the old myths, and well worth a look:

http://neversaynevergreyhounds.blogspot.ie/

https://www.facebook.com/NeverSayNeverGreyhounds/?fref=ts

In some areas you also might find fun lure-coursing available, which does not involve chasing a live animal and is a great outlet for the more athletic hounds. However, it can be demanding on the limbs so it's good to condition your greyhound a bit before throwing her into it!

Since you and your greyhound are living in close quarters, it is also important that you pay attention to her diet. If she is being fed a dry dog food that is high in processed protein (more than 20%), she is likely to begin to get restless and fidgety, as protein levels over 20% for a greyhound living a relatively sedentary life can have that effect. That would be the equivalent of putting yourself on an Olympic athlete's diet and sitting at a desk 5 days a week, 8 hours a day. No dog food will list the protein in their "analysis" charts as "processed protein", but that is what it is. Better to buy low protein or "mixer" dog food, and mix in your own fresh protein from mince meat (chopped beef), chicken thighs, sardines and more. Briefly put: don't feed your greyhound more than is needed for the exercise she is getting.

Wrap-up
Living in a city or town can give you plenty to think about. Although I have offered some detail, once you are well set up, it all just becomes second nature. It is perhaps sufficient access to exercise and toileting that is most important to a happy lifestyle, and it has to be an access that is daily, and in terms of toileting, several times a day. If you think you are not ready for this level of commitment yet, that's fine you are seeing it now and not three weeks after you have adopted a greyhound. After all, you can always help out at a rescue, look after someone's greyhound for a weekend, and perhaps even foster one for a short time. In the next chapter, I offer some tips for how to make this commitment a bit easier on you so that it is not a daily hassle, and also provide some background on different types of equipment so that you have at least a foundation upon which to start your new life with your new companion.

3 BASIC NEEDS OUT WALKING

"I always used the routine of a walk for re-grounding my dogs whenever we returned home from a trip or they were coming home from being in kennels. This was like a signal to them that everything was now returned to normal, and the deviation from the normal routine was now over, and the normal routine was now restarted. It always resettled them."
(Wendy W, Nottingham, UK; multiple greyhound owner)

Both you and your greyhound or greyhounds being well prepared for a walk is essential if you plan to enjoy yourselves. From the right equipment for your greyhound to the best clothing for yourself, and always having some essentials on hand, a little preparation can make walks go very smoothly. Although you might have a friend you visit who makes it look effortless when it's time to walk the dog, chances are that there is a bit of thought behind the appearance of her just leashing up doggie and breezing out the door without a care in the world. For example, in spite of collars, harnesses and leashes serving the same purpose in the countryside as well as the city, they have crucial importance in high traffic and dense population areas, where the pros and cons of different types of equipment could have life and death consequences. Even what you choose to wear and bring can even have a big impact on how the walks are experienced. So in terms of what is needed for taking walks, let's start with what YOU need first.

Humans: be prepared
The benefit of having specific jackets or coats expressly for walking your greyhound can actually help the walks to go smoothly. This is true not only because you always know that you have "walking things" you need in the pockets, but also because of the convenience if they are always hanging on

the back of the door you would normally go through to go out walking....and hanging right next to the leash. Of course, the right footwear for the weather should be there too. But let's get a bit more specific about this.

First, if you live anywhere but the desert, it's always best if you have a water-proof or water-repellent jacket, coat or outdoor vest <u>with a hood</u>. Having a hood means you do not need to carry an umbrella in case it rains, and that your hands are free for the leash and carrying that mug of coffee you need for those early morning walks.... Of course, if the hood has a small brim on it, that's even better...I admit I saw someone with such a hood not too long ago and I have been lusting after it ever since! The brim is useful for rain or snow, and even the glare of a brilliant winter sunset. All in all, however, a hood on your jacket or coat is always more handy than a hat, which can fall off or get blown off.

Just as important is water-proof or water-resistant footwear, always kept near the hooded jacket and the leash. From Crocs to fancy wellies or water-proof hiking boots, the idea here is that rain or the threat of rain should not be a factor in whether or not you take your greyhound out for a walk. This is especially so if you are living in an apartment and you don't have a small back garden: you need to be able to throw on what you need in an instant and just GO. I should add that this does not mean you need to spend a lot of money to "gear up". Considering the icky things a dog can sometimes encounter....or roll in....while out and about that can rub off on your clothing, it might be wise to find a hooded jacket or coat on sale somewhere or at a second hand shop.

No matter if you are using a hooded coat, jacket or outdoor vest, if there are lots of pockets, both outside and inside, they can be very useful. In them you can put dog treats, an extra house key, a pair of old garden gloves, a chocolate bar *(very important)*, a small travel pack of tissues or moistened wipes (for when you greyhound rolls in something absolutely disgusting), and don't ever forget to include your mobile phone. You will need your phone in case of an emergency, no matter if it's your greyhound's emergency or someone else's. You might wonder why on earth I suggest some old garden gloves....don't worry, you'll think of me the moment the need for them arises...... *"ooooohhh, so <u>that's</u> what she was talking about....."* But most important of all, those pockets MUST always be holding a good bit of spare change for that morning coffee or afternoon ice cream you so greatly deserve.

So the bottom line here is to simply be prepared. On those days when the weather can't quite decide what it wants to do, then if you are prepared there is nothing for you to worry about, as a hooded jacket or coat simply allows you to grab it, the leash and the greyhound, and breeze on out the door. Even for hot weather, having a sort of loose vest or even a waist purse (fanny pack) with various doggy needs in it can make walking go rather handily for you. Once you are out there walking, *there is plenty enough for you to have to manage without also not having prepared your own self.*

Collars and Harnesses
People might wonder why greyhounds are so special and need special collars. Well, although all pet greyhound owners think greyhounds are special anyway, the need for special collars has nothing to do with that. There really is a more practical reason. Greyhounds have such narrow heads that a normal dog collar can pop right off a greyhound's head very easily, even if you tighten the collar too much. They are <u>*very easy*</u> for a greyhound to back out of.

There are two types of collars that prevent this, and there are also "house collars". A lot of discussions can be found about house collars versus outside collars, martingales versus "fishtail" collars, and even the use of "head collars", which go by such name brands as Halti, Gentle Leader, Dogmatic and more. Here, we cover them one at a time and comment on their advantages and disadvantages.

House collars
These collars come in 2 or 3 varieties. One is in the form of very simple neckbands that your greyhound wears around the house only. It usually has no hardware protruding from it, such as a leash ring, and so it cannot get caught on anything, and is not designed to tighten when pulled, so it cannot choke your dog or get her caught on anything. The point of a house collar simply is meant to be something you can grab on to should you need to escort your greyhound in or out of a room or otherwise control her. Rarely these collars will have a small D-ring for a leash, just in case you need to move your dog by leash.

Another type is a single loop or noose that is slim or corded/rolled fabric or leather. It is worn loosely around the greyhound's neck, and again is only meant for moving a dog or taking hold of it. It really is a kind of noose, and you would not want to go out walking with it, as it really could choke your greyhound in an emergency.

The down side of using house collars at all is that it can be a constant inconvenience if you are often coming and going with your greyhound, or if you have children who often misplace the "outside" collar. Of course, if you have protrusions in your house that your greyhound's martingale collar could get stuck on, such as a radiator valve your greyhound is often sleeping near, maybe a house collar will be worth the hassle. Over the years, all the dogs who came through Orchard Greyhound Sanctuary never wore house collars, and I never had a problem with regular martingale collars. However, if you want "to be sure to be sure", then by all means do use a house collar.

Martingales
What great fun martingale collars can be, as they are usually made of fabric and are offered in a gorgeous array of patterns and colours. They are a sort of "indirect" choke collar, in that, IF they are fitted right, cannot come off the greyhound's head if the greyhound is pulling. People who don't properly fit their martingales - and almost all of them come with a slider for adjusting – often complain that they  pop right off their greyhound's head. Of course, your shoes also will fall off if they are tied loosely, but that is no reason to be opposed to shoes! There are plenty of videos on the web explaining how to properly fit a martingale.

They often come in different widths, too, and it can be important to avoid collars that are very wide, such as more than 6cm or 2 inches, since greyhounds can get into the habit of leaning heavily on the wider collars. Those collars less than 6cm or 2inches might be good for most greyhounds, though if you have a greyhound with a very long neck who is particularly good on the leash, then a wider collar can look quite elegant as well as be quite functional. Brass hardware is most desirable since it is stronger than nickel-plated, though these can come in different gauges or strengths. Martingales made with plastic fittings should be avoided as well as any metals that appear easy to bend. Collar-making is now a cottage industry in any countries where there are pet greyhounds and sighthounds in general, and there are many of them. To have a sample look at the variety available in martingales, have a look at (and don't hesitate to order from) any of these three sources:

Europe: www.kitschcollars.com

United States and Canada: http://www.2HoundsDesign.com

Australia: https://www.facebook.com/redhotpet/

And keep in mind that if you order a collar, you might also be able to order a matching leash at a length you require.

Fishtails
Classic racing collars, these can come in plain brown leather, a variety of coloured leather, and some even have some very fancy tooling, painting, or decorative studs on them. Their basic design prevents a greyhound being able to back out of them. 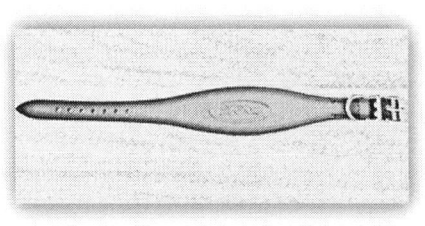 However, the collar does take up a lot of skin area of the neck. If it is worn day in and day out, it creates a perfect environment for skin irritations or a fungus to develop. If you are going to use a fishtail, make sure you remove it frequently or only use it for going out walking. Another warning is that because they are generally leather, some young greyhounds might find them well worth a chew!

Head collars
Often used as a solution for dogs who pull, there are many people who swear by these devices and others who swear at them. Different ones work on slightly different principles, but all of them revolve around have control of a dog's head. Rather than being fitted around a greyhound's neck, they are fitted around the head, much like a head collar or halter on a horse.

However, it is difficult for me to recommend these devices. I worked with Thoroughbred horses for many years, and knowing how much power and leverage one has with a 1200 pound (550 kg) horse when it is wearing a halter, it is worrying to also have that much power and leverage over a dog, even a largish dog, and especially a long-necked dog. The potential for abuse or injury seems great. Moreover, if your greyhound has a pulling problem, both you and your greyhound are bound to get a lot more out of a re-training effort than simply slipping an overly restrictive device on his head. However, developing a positive working relationship with one's dog is not everyone's priority and some people are only interested in instant results.

Harnesses
Many people use harnesses as an alternative to a collar, especially if their greyhound pulls. Some greyhounds do seem to stop pulling once a harness is tried, and people feel like they have greater control of their greyhound's body while at the same time avoiding the complications with collars. However, harnesses can also encourage a greyhound to pull, so they are not the end-all, be-all that some claim.

There are several matters to keep in mind, the first being to make sure you speak to several other greyhound owners who use harnesses about what their experience has been. They might end up telling you what brands to avoid and why, and offer you tips on fitting and other details. Simply getting the opinion of the sales person in a large pet store will rarely be as good as speaking directly to greyhound owners who use harnesses. This is because fitting a small-waisted, flat-ribbed, deep-chested greyhound to a harness is very different than fitting a pug or a spaniel, for example. People who actually use the harnesses can give you tips on how to keep your greyhound from slipping out of it since greyhounds can back out of some harnesses as easily as some can get out of regular collars. *Getting this hands-on advice directly from people who have been using harnesses for years is the best way to get sound information.*

One disadvantage to harnesses is that if your greyhound does get loose and has been exclusively using the harness, it might be difficult for other people to get hold of her in case of an emergency. With a loose greyhound, for example, most people will try to grab the greyhound by the collar or try to get a leash around her neck rather than snapping a leash onto the harness. If your greyhound is head-shy or hates being handled around the head, you can imagine this could be very problematic. So if you are going to use a harness, make sure you sometimes normalize her to a collar and leash, too, just for safety's sake.

Leashes
I like to think a leash should give the greyhound enough room to have a little sniff and yet not so short that you feel like your greyhound is underneath you. The leash needs to be long enough to extend out and yet short enough to quickly bring in to you if something arises. For example, you might be walking on a path or a narrow sidewalk and someone is headed your way with a baby carriage or is on a bicycle and they are not looking like they are willing to step aside even a little bit (and that's another issue). <u>You can put the leash handle in the hand from the opposite side from where the dog is, slide your other hand about half way down the leash and wrap it around your hand and pull your dog close to you. This can all be done in one seamless motion.</u>

In general, it's also good if the leash you use has some identification on it, even if it's just a phone number, and also is a bright colour so it is easy to locate, no matter if you are home or at a friend's house. Likewise, your leash should be able to be gathered up and put in a handbag or jacket pocket. Even "long leashes" or tracker leads, which are often slimmer than more conventional leashes, should be able to be gathered up and placed in a jacket or coat pocket. The reasoning behind this is simple: you will always need to know exactly where it is in case of an emergency, and this includes having quick access to it. Perhaps, for example, you have driven up to the gates of a dog park, and you figure you will just walk your greyhound to the gate by holding the collar and then let her loose: **please don't. Bring your leash with you, and don't leave it in the car**.

Extendable leads
At first glance, extendable leads might seem like a great idea, giving your greyhound room to explore, getting her in the HABIT of being away from your side yet still within your company. She learns to keep an eye on you, and that where you go, she goes. In spite of this, the down side of extendable leads has two main problems:

> *1) if the handle gets snapped out of your hands, the sound of it often results in a greyhound frightened by the noise, and will only make a loose dog run faster and longer as it follows behind them,*

clacking out an alarm and frightening them even further;

2) even if the handle is always under your control, it could be very easy for the cord or webbing to get caught in your greyhound's sensitive long legs, cutting off or slowing down circulation, or worse.

Conventional leash
I have a preference for keeping things simple: a one inch wide brightly coloured nylon leash, about 6 ft or 180 cm long, a simple handle at one end and a sturdy clip at the other. A leash this length is great for city walking, as it is, as mentioned above, short enough to quickly bring your dog in close to you should you need to, but long enough to let her investigate or step away from you should she not want to poo directly where you are walking. A shorter leash often can make you feel like the greyhound is constantly underfoot and in the way, and if she wants to step off the path into a slightly muddy area to toilet, and you don't want to step into the mud, a shorter leash is not helpful here.

Moreover, with a slightly longer leash you can have more control in an emergency. If something frightens or excites your greyhound and suddenly she becomes like a salmon on a line, <u>you can "wrap" yourself into the leash at hip level and lean back a little bit to prevent yourself from being pulled away or falling down</u>.

Long leashes (a must)
Sometimes called tracker or tracking leads, these are very handy leashes to have on hand and you really should own one as a matter of course. Coming in different lengths, from 5 meters to 10 meters and more, these simple basic leads are useful for recall training, for allowing your greyhound to have a greater sense of freedom, and for giving her more exercise than a walk on a conventional lead could. For example, even if you live in the middle of a

busy city where you dare not let your greyhound off leash, there is no reason why she cannot have more space to explore when you come across more open areas. Your walk through the city often includes plazas, green areas, sometimes canal paths, waterfronts, and more. If there are limited numbers of people around, there is no reason why you can't extend the long leash a bit and let your greyhound investigate those bushes, wade a little into the water, or have a brief run with you on an open green.

You will need to get used to manipulating a long leash, however, and _it will take a few outings with it to get the hang of it_. Four tips worth noting are:

1) tie a knot in the leash every two arm-lengths or so; these knots will prevent the leash from sliding through your hand should your greyhound very suddenly begin to pull;

2) about half way down the leash, make a knot that has a hand-size loop in it you can use as a handle; this will have a range of uses every day and particularly in emergencies;

3) when you are needing your greyhound to walk close to you but you want to keep the long leash on, learn to hold the long leash in gathered-up loops _that hang no further down than just above your knee_;

4) get into the habit of being able to quickly wrap the leash in your hand twice in order to further prevent it from running through your hand and giving you "rope burn".

Of course, the long leash is also wonderful to use if you are taking your greyhound on an outing to the beach or the countryside. If she is not yet ready to be off lead, or you are unsure if it is unsafe to let her off lead, you can simply clip on the long leash and let her have a lot more freedom than she normally would on your regular leash.

And one last little tip here: long leashes are sometimes sold at very high prices. If you want to make your own, you can purchase a few meters of 1in / 2.5 cm webbing and a leash clip, or just use the clip from an old, worn out leash. You can run the webbing through the clip end and make a knot to fasten it. From there you can, at the other end, make a handle from a looped knot, as shown on the right. After that, you can also add your knots and extra handle along the leash as stop points.

To muzzle or not to muzzle?
Before covering types of muzzles, it might be good to discuss the use of them to begin with. Unfortunately for those who believe muzzles are a must, I have a bad attitude towards them and never liked them. It always seemed to me that when a greyhound's racing days are over, muzzling days should be over too. Times have changed, and most people don't adopt their greyhounds two days off the track, still fresh with the buzz of racing and high on processed protein diets. After all, any dog fed over long periods on a dog food with a high per cent of processed protein can appear to be out of control; more about that subsequently. Most greyhounds are adopted from rescues who, to varying extents, have assessed their greyhounds and act as a transition space for adapting to pet status. I always found it ironic that the people who are most against racing are the ones who perpetuate the greyhound stereotype by insisting on muzzling their pet greyhound in public, no matter how long she has been a pet and how well behaved she is. It seems unfair.

Of course, if you have a greyhound who attacks other dogs, you need to use a muzzle while you are also working on the problem. I also wonder what "attack" really means, since I know many people will use the word "attack" when in fact their greyhound is just uncontrollably over-enthusiastic and needs to learn some basic manners. These greyhounds might need an experienced behaviourist who would be able to determine if unprovoked attacking really is what's taking place, and if your greyhound really needs a muzzle at all.

More pertinent to the town and city greyhound is when you might now and then encounter a loose dog who provokes your greyhound, and if muzzling your greyhound will prevent a fight. If a loose dog is provoking your leashed and muzzled greyhound, she doesn't have a chance at defending herself, especially if you have inadvertently dropped the leash and your greyhound has been cornered. You might have to see for yourself the damage an attacking dog can do to a muzzled greyhound. *It's unforgettable.*

Even if your greyhound really does nip other dogs, for example, keep in mind the muzzle is *only a band-aid* for that behaviour and not a solution. The muzzle is a temporary measure until you can train your greyhound some better self-control. Also, unless it's fitted just right, muzzles can come off. Of course muzzles can be used for legitimate reasons, such as when first exposing an unfamiliar greyhound to cats, small dogs or children or when working with an extremely difficult and aggressive greyhound around other dogs; some vets muzzle dogs who are being treated or lifted if injured. Even older books on greyhound adoption advise you to muzzle your greyhound the first week or so you own it, but in this day and age, when there are so many greyhound adoption programs and so much more assessment experience behind us, such advice is rarely needed to be followed. These books were written when many greyhounds were being adopted straight off the track. *The bottom line here is that the regular use of a muzzle will not solve a bad behaviour problem.*

All that being said, there are three basic types of muzzles. The first is a plastic muzzle that looks like a basket, comes in different colours and usually has some degree of padding on it. It allows the greyhound to drink water, and treats can be given through it. The second type is made of wire, often seen only at racetracks, and gives your dog the appearance of having just come from a Borg ship, if you have ever watched *Star Trek: the Next Generation*. The third is usually a sort of leather or imitation leather tube that fits over the dog's mouth, and prevents eating, drinking, and does not allow a greyhound to pant: please don't ever use this kind!

Muzzles might best be seen as _only_ provisional and stopgap safeguards, nothing more. The best policy is to invest some time and effort into training and re-conditioning.

Two other walking-related needs
Besides a proper collar and leash, or harness and leash, what other items might you need for walking your greyhound in towns and cities? There are some items which are pretty much required and others which are optional but very handy to have.

Poo bags!
First, you will need small plastic bags for picking up poo. Yes, it would be wonderful if greyhounds didn't poo at all, but they do, and cleaning up after them is part of the responsibility of having them. It's simply easiest to buy them in packets from a pet supply store. You can also try using biodegradable poo-bags or even biodegradable nappy/diaper sacks. And there are even small poo-bag dispensers which will fit handily in your pocket, clip on to your clothing or even attach to the handle end of your leash. The best way to pick up the poo – yes, the art of poo collection – is covered in Chapter 6.

Identification
We all know the benefits of microchipping, tags and contact information inked onto the inside of a collar. Microchipping is great if your greyhound gets loose and is gone for more than a day, since the finder would need time to get her scanned and access your contact information. *However, having ID tags is just as important.* After all, if you are in a park that is several acres or more and your greyhound gets loose or wanders off, someone at the other end of the park might find your dog and be able to ring you immediately, while you are still in the park searching. By only using the microchip for identification, this would not be possible. If your greyhound does disappear for more than a day, it is VERY good to always have on hand a photo that is clear, not too old and *most importantly is a full body side view* clearly showing markings and colouring. There's nothing as unhelpful as someone posting a photo of their lost dog, and the photo is a head-on image.

Closing comments
As you can see, preparedness is everything, both for you and your greyhound. You can even be prepared while on a tight budget, too, from picking up a suitable jacket or coat at a second-hand shop to making your own tracking lead. Also, think about if you live in an apartment, and your greyhound awakens you at 3:30am on a rainy night and desperately needs you to take her out. You might not be happy about it, but you will be less happy cleaning up diarrhoea from your favourite carpet. If you are always prepared, you can respond to your greyhound's urgent request to go outside by trudging to the door where the coat, leash and footwear are ready and waiting, knowing everything you need is there, knowing you will not need to look for things in a half-awake state. And as you stand out there

in the lonely night as it's starting to rain, the street lights beaming brightly down on your greyhound squirting out the worst diarrhoea you have ever seen, you will put your hand in your pocket and be so utterly glad to find not only the saved packet of mints you bought yesterday, but, thank God, the extra house key. It will feel like you won the lottery.

4 BASIC NEEDS AT HOME

"And a word from Monti Greyhound: he thinks that you should have a chapter in your book about creating a luxury environment for your Greyhound such as what type of sofas they like, pillows and lots of them, breakfast preferences, teatime treats, dinner requirements, foot and body massages, music preferences, special treats such as coconut cake, ale, toast, wood, shoes, plastic bottles, yoghurt, ice cream - any flavour etc. ..." (Lisa M, Drogheda Animal Rescue slave and Monti's servant)

Now Monti Greyhound mentioned above could be mightily disappointed to find out that I will not be advocating coconut cake and ale, but in this chapter I try to cover the basic practicalities at home and then some. There is certainly plenty to consider, and some of this chapter is covered in more detail in **Understanding Greyhounds**. Of course, the focus here is on an urban environment, and even though the basic needs of your urban greyhound are similar to that of a pet greyhound in the countryside, the exceptions are worth discussing. Coats are covered in Chapter 9, and fencing and gates were discussed in Chapter 2. Several miscellaneous items are included in this chapter as well.

Beds and bedding
Greyhounds have only half the body fat (17%) of most other types of dogs (34%) — such as Golden Retrievers or German Shepherds. They can very easily develop pressure sores, which are the canine equivalent of human bed sores, if they don't have a lot of padding in their sleeping area. Just throwing a blanket on the floor is not good enough. They need cushioning, and you can keep it simple or spend a lot of money on it. A very comfortable

bed is particularly a must for greyhounds who are walking on pavement quite a bit. People joke about what prima donnas their greyhounds are, but I suspect those are the same people who never had to treat an infected pressure sore.

Some greyhounds are perfectly fine with an old duvet folded in halves or quarters, depending on the size and loft. Others who, during their racing lives, have been bedded on lots of shredded newspaper, might think that shredding duvets can be a lot of fun. If you have a duvet cover that is good quality, this might deter shredding. For some greyhounds, you will want to avoid pillows filled with shredded foam, tiny Styrofoam balls, or any sort of feathers *(and wouldn't that last one be so much fun to rip to pieces, yes?)*. However, quiet and relaxed greyhounds have little interest in such silly behaviour, and are always happy for a soft bed which they generally have the good sense not to destroy. Generally this means a folded or cut down duvet made of "polyfil" (polyester stuffing) or even folded up pure wool blankets. Regarding the wool blankets: they don't hold doggy odours like synthetic blankets do, have lots of loft, and are easy to wash.

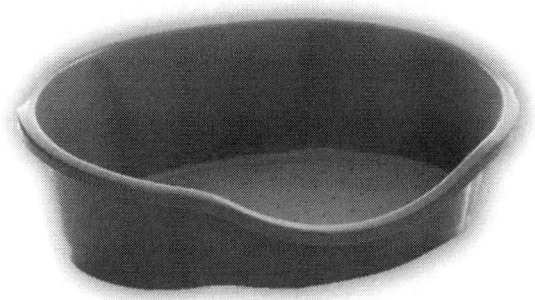

For the most part, a simple large oval plastic dog bed with old blankets and duvets in it is fine. Easy to clean and move around, it is very handy. Some companies make a softer sort of *fabric* bed, round/oval or square/rectangle shape with high rounded sides and some good cushioning in the middle. For these beds, you would need a blanket over it most of the time, as they can be difficult to clean since they cannot be put in the washing machine. They might need something absorbent placed under them since condensation can collect and eat away at the fabric that is touching the floor.

Overall, beds for sleeping should be slightly raised off the floor to avoid damp and drafts, out of the line of incoming drafts, and in a quiet place. Being in line with an incoming draft – such as an outside door that is used very frequently, can be worse than exposing your greyhound to the cold. The need to have a greyhound up off the floor and away from drafts can be found in manuscripts stretching back 500, 800 and 2000 years, so there is nothing new here about the importance of avoiding drafts. You can check for where the drafts are by placing the dog bed where you _think_ it's fine, and lie down on the floor yourself for 5 or 10 minutes to feel if there is a constant draft, or sit on the floor and light a candle and watch the flame. Keep in mind if your neighbour happens to peek in the window you might have some questions to answer..... And by "quiet place" I mean that if your house or apartment is on a busy street, then try to put the bed towards the back of the house, and not in the front room.

There is also the possibility of your greyhound sleeping in bed with you. Should your bed also be your greyhound's bed? Even if you live alone and have a king size bed, should you share it with your greyhound? There are pros and cons to this, enough for an entire chapter. Briefly, however, on one hand, it is natural for a greyhound to want to be up off the ground and out of drafts and near you. On the other hand, this can interrupt your sleep, although you might be able to restrict your greyhound to sleeping near the footboard. If you do this, be firm about it, as they often try to gravitate to the dead centre of the bed, where they magically become deaf and seem to be twice their kilos or pounds in sheer dead weight. Allowing your greyhound or any dog too much control of the bed can begin to make her possessive and actually get rather growly. So if you can't keep your greyhound near the footboard, then be forewarned here that you could soon start losing sleep and getting bossed around. If you don't plan to let your greyhound on your bed, make sure you provide her with a proper dog bed where it is in a comfortable and draft-free area.

If you have a house on two or more levels and your greyhound is allowed on all or some of them, then it is always good to have some sort of bedding available to her on each floor. For example, on the ground floor you will have a kitchen and living room. If you are likely to spend a lot of time in both, then either have a padded area or a dog bed (depending on space) available in both rooms. However, if your greyhound is allowed on a sofa or chair in the living room and it provides a view of the kitchen, then there is no need for extra bedding in the kitchen. Even if your greyhound is not allowed on the sofa in the living room, then just be sure to provide some padded, non-drafty resting space somewhere with a view into the kitchen. If you don't have a lot of space, even the space under a drop-leaf table, under the stairs, or in a corner of the room you don't use that often anyway will do. Convincing your greyhound to adjust to where you want her to sleep at night is dealt with in the next chapter.

Sustenance
This is just a brief review of the basics, and not a full blown discussion. The most basic rule is that most greyhounds need to be fed twice a day and need unlimited access to water. They need to be fed twice a day because their digestive systems cannot normally ingest all the food needed to sustain themselves in just one feeding. They also need unlimited access to water because they dehydrate easily, and many pinched and ribby greyhounds are not underfed, but underhydrated. Also, some older and well-rounded greyhounds might turn up their noses at a morning meal or just pick at it. *However, this is generally normal*, as they are old enough where their metabolism has slowed down and they don't actually need two full meals. Other than the older and well-rounded greyhounds, those who don't get two meals a day and/or have insufficient access to water will begin to deteriorate rapidly, even within several days. If your greyhound is in good condition and turns down a meal now and then, it often can simply mean she is just not that hungry. Greyhounds can be very good at self-regulating their food. Unlike the greyhound industry, individual greyhounds can be very good at self-regulation.

Exactly WHAT you choose to feed your greyhound can be as complicated or simple, as costly or inexpensive, and as controversial as you choose. There are lots of blazing arguments on the internet about dog foods and also various raw food diets. There is no point in reviewing all of them here, or advocating one dog food over another. Perhaps more useful would be to provide some basic information about what has been successful for dogs which have been in my own care. First, I never fed a purely raw meat diet because I always had too many dogs in my care and simply could not afford it nor the time it would have taken to get hold of it. So basically, I always have fed a base of plain dry dog food that has no preservatives or colourings and then I supplemented it. In fact, I would think of and treat the plain dry dog food as equivalent to how humans rely on bread as a base. I never fed a "complete" dry dog food because I want more control of what my dogs eat. I also am not averse to grains because the historical research I did on greyhounds shows that they have been eating grain products for many hundreds and even thousands of years, though I am careful not to give them white flour products or food with too much corn or maize.[5] There are more details about how I feed after this next section, which brings up an important matter regarding dry dog foods in general.

Protein levels
Perhaps the most important and useful feeding fact I learned here has to do with the protein per cent of dry dog food and its link to behaviour. This was mentioned in previous chapters but I expand on it here.

I noticed that when I initially would take in some greyhounds, and also when I saw greyhounds at some other rescues, they often seemed edgy and barking a lot. At first I could not understand why. They reminded me of when I had worked with high-level competition horses years earlier, and I remembered that even a 1% protein difference in a horse's food could be the difference between the horse being a rambunctious but manageable high-performance super-athlete or a twitchy, unfocused beast. Even reducing their protein intake by 1 or 2% made an observable difference in their ability to focus and be rideable. Too much protein could easily go to a horse's head. Once the food was changed, it could sometimes take up to two weeks to see the difference, *but there always was a difference.* I wondered if that also could be applied to dogs; after all, if racing greyhounds were fed about 28% protein to give them the stamina, energy, muscle growth and more to help them with racing, and if "resting" greyhounds were generally on 20% protein, then doesn't it follow that non-competing dogs need less protein?

This problem with protein levels seemed to only be limited to dry dog food, and not tinned food or real meat or fish. It is still not clear to me if the problem is with the preservatives needed for high protein dry dog food, or if it is the processed protein itself. I systematically experimented with this over the years on the dogs in my care, and quickly observed that **protein directly from meat or fish did not have this affect.**

Of course, it might affect some dogs more than others, and if you have only one or two greyhounds and there are no behaviour problems at the higher protein levels, that's great. The main point to keep in mind is that if you have a greyhound with a behaviour problem *and* he is on a high protein

---

[5] Corn in dog food is a controversial subject, and is a separate discussion on its own.

diet, try lowering the protein first and see if the behaviour begins to "break up" on its own accord. **There is little point in trying to get through to a dog who is too high to focus.** It also should go without saying to avoid dry dog foods that have a large amount of preservatives or colouring agents in them, as it is not clear what role they play in behaviour problems.

Food: amounts, supplements, tips and schedule
I stopped paying attention to the "suggested" feeding amounts on the back of dog food bags years ago since it's difficult to know if what they suggest actually can apply to low-bodyfat greyhounds or not. A good rule of thumb is that if your dog is underweight, and he's hungry all the time, feed him more! As long as your greyhounds' ribs, hip bones, and spine are fairly well covered, that's quite ok. My other rule of thumb is approximately half a litre (about half a quart) of dry dog food per greyhound per feeding, a little more for the bigger ones, a little less for the smaller ones. I like to feed them enough so that they feel satisfied, but might even leave a small bit in the bowl.

The routine I used when my sanctuary was in full swing was in the mornings I would "free feed" the dogs here. This meant modest portions of dry food, sometimes coated lightly with something like sunflower oil, broth from last night's cooked meat, yogurt, or some other tasty and healthy liquid – maybe even beaten raw eggs – are spooned into feeding bowls. If you have several dogs, you might put down maybe one or two more bowls than there are dogs. This discourages food aggression as well as a new dog getting stressed about finding that one last free bowl. It also ensures the shy ones to have their fair portion. There was never a very precise time to feed them in the morning, and this conditioned the dogs to be a bit flexible about feeding time.

In the evenings I'd give warm meals, the food bowls set up <u>at least</u> a meter away from each other. <u>*A warm meal at night can settle a greyhound down nicely for the evening, especially a newly arrived greyhound.*</u> Each would be given about half a litre/quart of dry food mixed with a handful of meat or fish, a handful of porridge oats and hot water: in other words, an evening stew. *The food was not at all soaked in hot water*; instead, the hot water was poured over it all, it was stirred and immediately put in front of the dogs. It is important for the food to maintain a good degree of crunch for the sake of dental care, the crunching good for the gums and scraping the teeth somewhat (more on dental care towards the end of this chapter).

The meat or fish was shredded or cut into very small pieces so they could not pick it out from the dry food, The hot water poured over it made a sort of gravy that infused somewhat into the dry dog food. Again, a warm meal at the end of an active or stressful day can settle and relax a new greyhound and further foster quiet and calm behaviour in an established greyhound.

The above is all very adaptable to having a single dog or just a few. By free feeding and leaving out food from the morning time, then if you are working during the day or need to go out for several hours, then your greyhound or greyhounds are not left with no food whatsoever. If they are genuinely hungry or even a little bored, they will crunch some food. Since it is not high-value food to them, there is unlikely to be any fighting over it. Just the knowledge of having food available if needed is great for preventing stress. And if you are delayed in coming home, you at least know there is something left out which can be eaten: no one is going to starve if you are 45 minutes or 2 hours late.

As for food supplements, there is no end to what you might add to your dog's diet for good health and overall wellbeing. Trying new foods in small amounts first is a good idea in order to see if the supplement agrees with your dog's digestive system, or to give your greyhound's system time to adjust. One supplement I always gave and still give regularly was uncooked porridge oats flakes (oatmeal): good for skin and coat; good for the immune system; good for relaxing the central nervous system.

WATER!
Greyhounds dehydrate very easily, and once dehydrated they can quite easily fall deeper and deeper into profound dehydration, *the end result being death*. Simply put, dehydration thickens the blood, and among other things, makes it more difficult for the heart to pump, and for the lungs to deliver oxygen to the bloodstream. Rather than constantly replenishing a small bowl several times a day, there are benefits to using a very large bowl or small bucket and topping it up once a day. In that way, you can gauge how much water your dog or dogs usually drink daily, and will be able to see when there has been an increase or reduction in intake. Even if you have

been away and left your greyhound at a boarding kennel, and she appears thin when you collect her, it might be wise to focus more on providing water as soon as you return home rather than food. *Keep in mind greyhounds are more likely to drink fully when there is a large amount of water in front of them rather than a small bowl.*

Stay inside or the great outdoors?
One of the saddest things to see is a dog who is kept outside 24/7, chained to a miserable little doghouse, and with nothing to do. We hate that image, and don't want our dogs to experience anything even remotely similar to one of those poor dogs. As a result, many of us limit the amount of time our greyhounds are outside unattended in our back gardens. Even leaving your greyhound alone inside can be a challenge to some, but the first rule of thumb when adjusting your greyhound to be left alone *inside or out* includes 4 basic conditions:

> 1) make sure she is tired (from a long or active walk, for example)
> 2) give her something to do while you are out (a kong, a bone, etc.)
> 3) restrict her to one part of the house unless you *must* confine her to a crate
> 4) keep the radio on for company (no death metal or headbanger music, please)

With the first point, this is just to take the edge off her. If you don't have time for a 50 minute walk, then take her on a 15-20 minute *very quick* walk or jog. Regarding the second point, do not offer the kong or bone until you have one hand on the door handle to leave. Once you hand it to your greyhound, she has to decide if she wants to cry and act out, or work on a goodie. The goodie usually wins. This gets her in the habit of *actually liking it* when you leave. As for the third point, ideally you don't want your greyhound to feel like she is overly restricted, so locking her in the utility room could result in a bad reaction to it. Instead, maybe give her the run of the kitchen and another commonly used room, but not the entire house. If she is a dog who has arrived to you as very destructive, then a large crate should be used, but it should be comfortably bedded and not set up in a back hallway or back room. When you are home and if the crate door is left open, she just might enjoy resting in, especially if you drape 2 or 3 sides of it with a sheet and thus make it like a little cave. And leaving on the radio means human voices and maybe even a soothing or "easy listening" atmosphere. As her reaction to you leaving dwindles to little reaction at all, you can then begin to reduce the degree to which you apply these four suggestions. There's nothing that feels as good as having to run out the door for a last-minute reason – maybe even an emergency – and knowing you can leave with your dog or dogs in the house and all will be well on your return.

There are also some advantages to our greyhounds learning to enjoy being outside to some degree, and below is a bit of food for thought presented as several scenarios where you might want to leave your greyhound outside, and for her to enjoy being outside:

- it is a gorgeous sunny day, not too cool or too hot, not a cloud in the sky, and you need to run an errand that will take maybe an hour; you live in a safe area, and what a pity to leave the greyhound cooped up in the house when she could be outside enjoying the sunshine;

- there are workmen in the house, going in and out the front door; the noise they are making and the coming and going is disturbing, and your greyhound could easily run out the front door to get away from it all;

- someone is coming to the house who is allergic to dogs or perhaps is fragile or otherwise cannot be around dogs for a legitimate reason;

- you regularly have to be away from the house for hours at a time, and so when the weather is beautiful, it would be healthier for your greyhound to be outside taking in the sun and fresh air; might a friendly neighbour or friend or relative let her in at some point?

- your carpets are being shampooed or some otherwise heavy cleaning is going to take place in the house and it is best if your greyhound is not underfoot;

- there has been an accident or emergency where you are delayed coming home for several hours but you have left your greyhound inside: you can ring your neighbour who has the key to your house and get them to open the back door to let your greyhound out when you know you might be home in an hour.

Now all of these are highly likely situations, and having a greyhound who does not at all mind going outside would be a handy convenience. It might take a little bit of thinking to get your greyhound accustomed to going and staying outside even for short periods. However, getting your greyhound used to being left outside is something you should start out with slowly and then build on. Of course, it might be easier still if there is a companion dog.

Now it might be that your greyhound presently thinks of your back garden as a bad-weather, or early morning and late-at-night peeing and pooing place. Perhaps you don't spend a whole lot of time in your back garden anyway. It would be good to begin to change your greyhound's idea of the back garden from a place for toileting to a place to enjoy and hang out in. To do this, you just need to lead the way, doing so in steps. At first, the initial step would entail a few weeks or less of going outside with your greyhound *and closing the door to inside behind you*. Start thinking of your garden as an outside room that is as integral to the house as the kitchen.

Hopefully you have a garden chair, which you should place a bit more than halfway back from the back door, and you are going to sit down and read a magazine or book, make a shopping list, or write brilliant poetry on the glories of being a greyhound owner *(Monti would like that)*. What's important here is that your greyhound cannot get back inside and your sitting in a chair signals to her *"we are staying here now, at this place."* Of course, by going and standing at the back door, and maybe even barking at you, your greyhound might be signalling to you *"oh no we're not….we belong INSIDE. Now get over here and open the door."* You remaining in the chair then signals to her *"nope, we are here now, in this outside room."* Giving your greyhound something that will take a while to chew on will help her to adjust to this new use of the back garden. If she is into toys, a new toy would be a nice diversion too.

The next step will be sometimes getting up and walking to one place or another within the garden, but still staying within the garden. This is to get her used to you getting out of the chair but not leaving. From here, this can graduate up to going in the house and closing the door behind you to get a treat for her and a glass of water for you…..then going back outside again, door closed. The message here for her is *"I DO go into the house without you, BUT I return with a treat, so me going into the house without you turns out to be a goody run."*

As your greyhound adjusts to this, you can stay in the house or be away from the house all together for longer and longer periods, always returning to remind her that she is not being abandoned. If she does begin to react too much to your leaving, then reduce the number of minutes you are in the house without her, or dial back even further and repeat the last step for a few more days. Always leave the chair well into the garden, as this is, to her, the same as furniture in the living room, and it signals your potential presence *(no, a scarecrow of you is not a good idea)*. Eventually, this should all be able to evolve into you wanting her to be outside for one reason or another, and using what ever key word you want for the back garden, stepping out the back door with her, handing her a treat that will take a while to gnaw on, and then leaving.

Of course the weather does not always cooperate with us, and we are unlikely to make much progress if it's pouring rain or bitterly cold. But, for example, if you know you are going out for several hours and the weather is fair but with the possibility of rain, you still can make this work for you. Put another way, you might feel great leaving your greyhound indoors as you leave for an errand that will take several hours, but if an hour after leaving the sky clears and the weather becomes glorious, your greyhound will have lost all that fresh air and sunshine time, and you will come home to a greyhound just dying to go OUT for a proper walk instead of dying to come in. This is worth keeping in mind if you are at times likely to come home exhausted.

All this means it would be great to have a small shed or cabin for your greyhound. If you already have something like a garden shed, reserve one section in it for your greyhound. She will need to be up off the ground and free from drafts. In this case, the easiest thing to do is put a standard pallet on the ground inside, throw some old carpeting over it (so toes don't get caught between the slats) and place an oval, hard plastic dog bed on top of it. The open side of the dog bed should not be in direct line with the door to the shed, to avoid getting hit by drafts. Put a few washable blankets or duvets inside the plastic bed, put your garden chair in there on a rainy day and do some reading or list-writing. In other words, brainwash your greyhound into thinking this is a room within the greater "outside room" that is your garden, maybe even an extra greyhound bedroom. Bring a cup of tea or coffee with you, have some dog treats in your pockets, and once she is in the bed, hand her one now and then. You are giving her a larger sense of "home space" and the back garden and shed just become extensions of the house itself. I know of one greyhound who enjoys her "outside bedroom" so much that when the house is getting a bit hectic, she actually _asks_ to be let outside and goes straight to her own private den. It is not a place of abandonment, but a place of comfort, quiet and relaxation.

None of what I have said here is to support the idea of leaving your greyhound outside 24/7 or even more than a few hours daily. This is also written with the knowledge that you might not feel your greyhound is safe left outside, and could be stolen or somehow hurt by outsiders: that is completely understandable. If you think your greyhound will be in danger, then leave her inside while you are away from home.

However, if security is not an issue, then it still will be worth conditioning her into learning to be in the "outside room" sometimes, whether you are home or not. Perhaps if you have a nice neighbour who keeps an eye on things, then during those weeks when you are going to be particularly busy for some reason, your greyhound will be better off outside for some days or half-days than inside in good weather. Even if your neighbour can let her out an hour before you come home, it helps with the flow of things. You will find there is something calming and even reassuring about driving home exhausted from a long day, knowing that you will go into the house, open the back door, make a cup of tea, and sit down on the sofa with your best friend to recover from the day together and without the pressure of having to immediately take her for a walk.

Coat, nails and teeth
You can make the care of your greyhound as simple and inexpensive or as complex and costly as you want. Here, some simple and easy tips are offered that you can do at home and with little fuss. If you want to do more, that's fine, you can build on this. Since you are walking your greyhound in traffic areas every day, however, you can't really be taking your greyhound to the groomer's for a shampoo everyday. No matter, there still are ways to keep your greyhound fresh as a daisy and otherwise in good form.

Coat

You have to imagine that if you are out walking in traffic every day, your greyhound's coat is picking up as much car exhaust, pollen, and pollution as your clothing and your own skin and hair. However, since most of us take showers and wash our clothes regularly, then all those pollutants and irritants are generally not an issue. It's a different story for your greyhound, and there is something simple you can do on a daily or almost daily basis to address what ever might have settled on and maybe into your greyhound's coat.

A simple wipe-down the moment you come in the door from a walk is easy enough. It might take two minutes at the least and five minutes if you want to linger. This can be done with great convenience by either leaving a small bowl of tepid water and a facecloth somewhere near the door you walk in when returning, or simply having a facecloth ready at the kitchen sink. If you choose to have a small bowl of water, adding a few capfuls of cider vinegar to it can freshen up your greyhound and also act as a deterrent for fleas and other parasites. Soaking your dog in it can affect the pH balance of your greyhound's skin, and act as a more robust deterrent, but for now, just a basic wipe-down is all we are looking for. And by the way, the vinegar smell will evaporate in less than 5 minutes.

You can begin at the face and work your way back, making sure you wipe the inside of the ears and under the collar, then detouring at the shoulders to go down the legs and even wipe down the pads and between the toes: you might be surprised at what you find! Make sure to do the undercarriage, up inside the thighs, down the back legs and back feet, and even the tail. *The more often you do it, the more skilled you become at it.* Doing this is going to have four additional benefits:

1) *it will have long term benefits to your greyhound's coat, picking up dead hair and skin and making it soft and glossy;*

2) *there will be less dog hair around the house and on your clothing and furniture;*

3) *wiping down your dog is the human equivalent of the mother dog cleaning her puppies, and this is likely to intensify your bond;*

4) *in the event of an injury, your greyhound will now be well used to you handling every part of her body.*

The benefits are so great, there in fact is little reason NOT to do wipe-downs.

This is only going to be of limited use if you have a greyhound with a very thick coat during shedding season. It will help somewhat, but can't really address the entire shedding problem. There are some greyhounds, especially white ones, who can shed so much, the hair coming out in clumps, that you are certain something is wrong and the greyhound is going bald. The only way to deal with this is daily or near-daily grooming or several weeks with a shedding brush. This is a tool with a handle for holding it and then a rectangular pad with stiff wire needles in it…..which will make your greyhound jump out of her skin it you are too rough with it! The other option is any one of a number of shedding gadgets with names like Shedmonster, Furgopet and Furminator. This last item is quite expensive, by the way, but does a great job.

Nails
Yes, I know: the idea of cutting your greyhounds nails is about as appealing to you as eating worms….in fact, you can at least wash worms down with a glass of wine. But you don't really have to feel that way. Once you have started wiping down your greyhound regularly, even greyhounds who are over-sensitive about their feet might let you give it a try. More about the hyper-sensitive greyhounds further on. Some ex-racing greyhounds have terrible nails, pointing in the wrong direction, or so thick they look like dinosaur talons, or sometimes sticking out straight from the toe instead of curling towards the ground. Gruesome. No wonder you prefer the worms.

Some might say that walking on concrete or any kind of pavement wears down the greyhound's nails. However, this varies according to surface and to the hardness of the individual greyhound's nails. Basically, you can start by determining if the nails need to be clipped. Have your greyhound standing up as normal on a hard floor, and see if you can slip a piece of paper between the floor and the nail. If you can't, the nails need clipping. Most important is to purchase nail clippers *which have a guard on them that prevent you from taking off more than a sliver*. **This is crucial.**

To get your own confidence up, and to instil confidence in your greyhound, get in the habit of picking up her leg while she might be on the sofa with you while watching tv. Move your hand to the foot and get used to just feeling her toes and nails, maybe massaging or pressing the pad of one toe, and if you can, move or wiggle the nail on that toe a tiny bit, just so she feels some movement and handling.

After you have done this for a few nights, bring the clippers with you and go through your usual motions of massaging and handling the foot. With your other hand, hold the clippers near the foot while you are doing this. You can even open and close them several times so that you get used to being in this position, with one hand on the foot and the other holding clippers. Once you are comfortable with that, you can even hold the clippers up to or against a nail, and open and close them a few times without nipping anything at all. Eventually your confidence will build and you will become impatient or bored with this baby-steps approach.....and will make the effort to clip the tiny tip of an easy nail. That's great. You'll think _"that wasn't so hard! what was the big deal?"_

There are even rotary tools you can purchase that will more or less file your greyhound's nails, though the noise of the motor and the sensation of constant vibration might bother some dogs. No matter if you are using clippers or a rotary tool, start with the easy nails, the white ones (if there are any) which are undistorted, non-dinosaur nails, and slowly work your way up to the more intimidating ones. This also goes for the dew claws, on the inside of the leg. Sometimes one dew claw can look like something from a horror movie, and the other is demure and simple. Start with the simple one. The more you do this, the more your greyhound will get used to you handling her, and the more you handle her feet, the more confident you will be.....and then the more confidence she will have in you.

For greyhounds who have a real phobia about their feet, be sympathetic. You have no idea why they are that way and what they have been through. It might take you months to even be allowed to handle the feet at all. You can start with leg massages, and slowly, very slowly, work your way closer and closer to the toes over a matter of weeks. Don't be in a hurry. If your greyhound objects, then back up to the place you were the day before, and stay there for a few days, then try again, only in the most subtle way. In the meantime, if she really needs her feet clipped desperately, then your vet can administer a sedative and do it quickly. However, it is best that *you* work on this with your greyhound, since you could need her to allow you to handle her foot in an emergency.

Teeth

This is a subject one could write pages about, and of which there is enormous information on the internet and in books and magazines. There is no point in reinventing the wheel here, but it might be a good idea to make a few main points. Former racing greyhounds can at times tend to have dreadful teeth, though it is more environmentally caused than genetic: often the food given to racing greyhounds is soft and sloppy, and this is not at all good for their teeth. You can think of dental care in terms of two levels of care: there is preventive home care and then veterinary care. And then within each of them there are two aspects.

preventive home care –

> dietary: *you can make sure your greyhound regularly eats foods which exercise the gums and scrape the teeth naturally, such as not over-soaking dry dog food, providing real marrow bones, and adding plaque-removing additives to the meal*

> direct intervention: *this means brushing your greyhound's teeth regularly, possibly using a meat-flavoured doggy toothpaste with either a dog toothbrush or a rubber finger cover that has little nodules on it.*

veterinary care –(be sure to see cautionary note below)

> scale and polish: *your greyhound is unconscious for this procedure, which means plaque removal and then a polishing of the teeth to keep the surface smooth; your greyhound needs to be anaesthetized for this procedure, which is done with a small electric dental instrument;*

> tooth removal: *also requiring anaesthetic, this is when the teeth are just too decayed to save; a tooth or sometimes many teeth get removed, and the greyhound usually recovers from it and should be well able to eat fairly normally within 24 hours.*

Cautionary notes

Greyhounds *can die* from the wrong anaesthetic or the incorrect anaesthetic procedure, *so make sure the vet clinic you are using is a vet clinic that has been recommended to you from another sighthound owner or convinces you of their expertise in this area.* Another caution is that some vets are more "enthusiastic" to remove teeth than others, or, to put it the opposite way, some vets would rather pull less teeth and conserve as many as possible. For example, if a tooth is looking like it is at the beginning of unstoppable decay or rotting, some vets will remove it even though it might take another year or more to significantly progress; however, another vet might prefer to wait and be as non-invasive as possible, only removing the very worst teeth. There are pros and cons to these views.

Outside Influences Causing Fear

Fireworks, thunder and lightning, sirens, the sounds of gunfire, construction noise and more can be very upsetting to our sensitive greyhounds. Not all of them will react badly, but some are bound to. It is a different type of fear than separation anxiety. First of all, finding the right balance regarding *what to do* and *what **not** to do*, and secondly, what our expectations are for reducing that fear, are both very important to making progress.

Although we might be tempted to soothe and reassure our quivering, salivating sighthound in the same way we would a small child, most of the time their fear or anxiety is too great for such efforts to make a difference.....and might even make things worse. Dogs who are in fear want to hide and feel somewhat removed and safe from the noise. They don't need to be overstimulated with a lot of constant petting and chatter. Not only can that tend to overstimulate them, *but it also is not helping them to learn how to deal with this problem*. We have to remember that some fearsome noises can start when we are not home, and so your hound would do well to learn how to cope with it a bit better. **It is up to us to show them how.**

There are a lot of products for sale that claim to help dogs deal with stress. Even though none of them help your greyhound to bond better with you or to actively learn how to deal with the fear, they can indeed be thought of as aids, as *something in addition to* basic coping behaviour your greyhound needs to learn. Your first step in dealing with this does not necessarily mean you have to go out and buy about $100, €100 or £100 of various aids for your greyhound, from a "thundershirt" to DAP diffusers and various calming aids. First, try _yourself_. I will say this again:

First, try _yourself_.

This does not mean these various aids don't help at all, but it is better if _first_, you and your greyhound together begin to learn how to cope with the fear. When you see the extent to which your own _unaided_ efforts are helping, _then_ you can decide which aid might be the next best step. We will return to this shortly

Remembering that frightened dogs seek a safe place to hide, you could start by making a little cave or safe place for your greyhound somewhere in the house. It could be in part of your bedroom closet, in a corner of a spare room under a table. If it is under a table, drape a blanket or duvet (not a sheet) over most of it _so that the noise is partly deadened and absorbed by the blanket._ On the closet floor or under the table (or where ever) make sure you put down something like a folded up duvet and your own laundry in there - old sheets, t-shirt, whatever - so she has your scent with her. You can coat her, too, if it will not make her feel too warm, OR put one of your own old t-shirts on her, so that she is surrounded by your scent.

Then, if possible, sit close to where she is and just watch tv or read or do something normal. _You don't need to convince her with words that everything is ok, because if you simply provide for her and are present for her, she is beginning to learn that in spite of the noise, you are there and nothing happens._ The idea is not to have her blank it out of her head, but for her to learn something. So she might still shake, but it will be less shaking than if you did nothing. When the fearful thing happens again, and then again after that, _this is where the learning process comes in_. By the third of fourth time, she will ready to know what to expect from you, and her reaction should be even a little improved. At night, let her sleep under your bed or under a table near your bed or in your bedroom closet...or you could make a little "fort" for her that has something over her head that will also deaden the noise.

Dogs learn through repetition, so you might never get her to be completely relaxed, but at least a bit less fearful. This is going to help her for the times you are not home! It will lessen the chances of her developing a more serious fear anxiety. Before you go out, you can always make sure she has access to her cave, so that when something scary happens, she know exactly where to retreat to. Louise C from Dublin describes how she also adds, for example, extra noise in the house and does use a mild calming agent:

> *Christine and Dolly do well on Kalm Aid, no lasting effects...a little more chilled than normal...and I hang a blanket over the kitchen table and have a duvet in there so they can hide under there in the dark. I turn the heating up, put the washing machine on, play a radio, turn up the TV and sleep on the floor with them sometimes.*

It's good to be prepared for other, unexpected fear reactions, too. One person I know recently described coming home to her sometimes-fearful greyhound hiding in the shower stall, somewhere he never goes. Through driving rains and high winds, he is always on her bed when she comes home. However, he did not want to leave the shower stall when she first returned home, and when he eventually did, he lay down on the bathroom floor close to the shower stall. Not shaking or having his tail between his legs, just why he was doing this was a mystery. His owner later found out that her landlord had allowed a workman into her apartment when she was out, but had never told her this was to happen. Being fearful of strangers, the shower stall was, to him, <u>the best hiding place he could find</u>. Even after his owner had returned home, however, he initially felt that it was safer to lie close to the shower, "just in case". Once he was satisfied all was well and the threat was no more, he returned to normal behaviour. This is a perfect example of what dogs want and need when they feel threatened.

Chapter wrap-up
So here you have had some background information on the basics of home care. No doubt this chapter could have been three or four times as long, as information and new ideas and products are constantly entering mainstream dog-ownership. Basic common sense and a little resourceful thinking can go a long way in figuring out small problems that occur, and there is a lot you can do yourself, especially in terms of preventive care. Money can buy you a lot of advice, but common sense should not have to be for sale.

For example, someone I know had three different behaviourists come to their home to watch their greyhound constantly pacing in their rather large kitchen. No one could understand it. I was asked to put in my own 2 cents. It turns out the poor greyhound was only looking desperately for a place to lie down that was comfortable, and not the bare floor, but was still in the kitchen, where everybody else was most of the time. Her downstairs bedding was in the next room, around a corner, far from sight of the kitchen. I brought her bedding into a corner in the kitchen and……the pacing stopped. Imagine. The dog never needed a behaviourist after all. Common sense is not so common sometimes.

This leads into the next chapter, which is about basic training ideas. Often you can set up your greyhound's environment so that she settles into it organically and ends up needing very little formal training. As one friend put it: "my two greyhounds have a big back garden to run and play in , and go for 30 minute walks twice a day. Other than that, they are horizontal with their legs up in the air. Why do I need training classes? They're great as they are!" Sounds easy, yes? Well, it can be if you set up your greyhound to succeed.

5 BASIC TRAINING OR RULES OF THE ROAD

"These past two years living in the city, my two hounds and I learned to evolve as a team. Not having a garden pushed me to find a more accurate communication with them. The city made me find the subtle words and body language and gestures to get through to my two hounds' personalities...the city is too fast-paced and many of the streets too narrow to not take the time to find a flowing way to communicate."
(Marie H, Paris and Montpelier, France; multiple greyhound and sighthound owner)

Greyhounds and similar hounds tend to be larger than many city dogs, and as such, need some manners and good reflexes in order to negotiate city life. It's your responsibility to train them, to condition them, to help them adjust to the challenges that this lifestyle brings. Having a greyhound in a town or city environment can be a lot easier if you start teaching her some basic cues at home which will come in handy in a wide range of situations, including emergencies. Here, the word *cue* instead of *command* is used very deliberately. The fact is that *commanding* your greyhound to do anything at all is being rethought by training and behavioural specialists. If you think about it, the skills needed for negotiating busy streets and all the distractions that come with it really require <u>*more of a cooperative signalling than commanded obedience*</u>. Let me say that again:

*the skills needed for negotiating busy streets
and all the distractions that come with it
really require
more of a cooperative signalling than commanded obedience.*

By cooperative signalling, I mean using actions, body language and sometimes tone of voice that your greyhound can understand instead of snapping out an order. For example, *commanding* your greyhound that everything is fine in spite of the fire engines that just went screaming past you does not really make sense. Slightly shortening the leash, bringing your greyhound closer to you, and laying your free hand reassuringly on your greyhound's back as you continue walking makes a lot more sense than snapping out "Hanzi, **heel**!". This is brought up repeatedly throughout.

There are several very easy and simple cues, and they can be worked on a few at a time or one by one, depending on your own comfort level, your greyhound's comfort level, and what your local circumstances require. By *what your local circumstances require* I mean that for some people, teaching your greyhound one sort of cue might be more immediately important than another: if your walks have you crossing a busy road every day with your somewhat fearful greyhound, working on that is going to be more important to work on right away than teaching her not to exuberantly jump at people. And as mentioned above, some of this cue work will rely more on your own body language than actually speaking, though tone of voice will be important too.

You might notice there is no suggestion here about signing up for training classes. That's because there is a lot to be said for doing as much as you can on your own. *This increases your bond with your greyhound, and your greyhound's bond with you.* There is quite an advantage of getting started at your own pace and according to your own schedule as well as your greyhound's capacity. There also could be something you would like and maybe even need to work on again for several days or weeks in a row instead of forging ahead with the training class's next planned exercise and the exercise after that. Being able to manage your greyhound at this level is also confidence-building for both of you and could be very important in the event of an emergency. Let's get started.

Cues versus commands
Many of us have two images of walking a dog in our heads. There is the dog who is straining on the leash, pulling the ground away with his front legs and shoulders so powerfully that any self-respecting, sledge-pulling Siberian Husky would be sick with envy. You see it in all types of dogs, from

Chihuahuas to Great Danes, and the bigger the dog, the more demanding it is on the person. Then there is the person walking along the path with a dog on a leash that is not taut, but instead is almost loosely hanging, and it all seems so effortless, the owner could almost read a book while doing it….though being online via a smartphone is almost the same thing. *We all want that second image*…unless of course you are training for the Iditerod Great Sled Race.[6]

There are several basic cues to suggest here, but they can only be taught from a reasonable starting point. The starting point is that normally, your greyhound walks on the leash fairly well most of the time, maybe pulls a small bit (especially when first starting out walking, out of excitement), but generally is under control. Perhaps sometimes your greyhound really does pull under certain circumstances, and that is what we are looking to address in this section with some cues. If you have a greyhound who is really yanking your arms out of your shoulder sockets, that's something else, and we discuss that a bit later in the chapter.

The STOP cue
There is no doubt in my mind that this is the most important thing you can teach your greyhound. It is a foundation cue, and if you never teach your greyhound anything else at all, at least teach her this. It can be used for the most simple everyday occurrences all the way to urgent crises. It is the easiest cue to teach. It means "stand still, don't pull on the leash, just stay here with me right now." You begin by expecting your greyhound to "hold" the stop for 5 seconds, then 10 seconds, then 30 seconds, then more. It will teach your greyhound that words and actions have meaning, and it will teach a little bit of self-control. The self-control your greyhound learns from this will spill over into other parts of her life. Here is a short list of when you might use the STOP cue:

- STOP I have to tie my shoe
- STOP I have to give directions to these people
- STOP I have to help this person who just fell
- STOP I just fell and can't have you pulling me
- STOP I am putting things into or taking them out of the car…maybe

---

[6] Well worth learning about! Known as "The Last Great Race on Earth", see http://iditarod.com/

> even the baby…

and, if something frightens your greyhound and the leash gets snapped out of your hand:

- STOP I am coming to pick up the leash

In this last situation, although some greyhounds might keep moving away from you, others might feel reassured at the familiar word and respond to it as a reflex, giving you just enough time to catch up. What to do if your greyhound does get loose or even lost is covered in Chapter 8.

There are two cues to give your greyhound when you want her to stop. When you first begin teaching it, by the way, you will not expect her to stand for too long, even if she is very good at it or does not seem to mind. At first, just getting her *in the habit* of stopping when she is cued to do so is the main goal. From there, you can build on length of time.

The first time you want to work on this, take your greyhound Flora out for a walk, and look ahead of you, and decide where on the path or the road you want to stop. As you approach it, you can begin to slightly lean back and just make 2 or 3 short tugs on the leash (not yanking!) and say **Flora, STOP** at the same time. As you stop walking, shorten up the leash and firmly stand still and tall, shoulders square and not looking down at her. The first few times might feel a bit uncoordinated, but by the 6th or 7th time you should feel a bit more natural and your greyhound will have a very good idea of what to expect. *Everyone gets better at something through repetition.*

After you have successfully done this a few times, once your greyhound stops, see if you can loosen your hold on the leash a little bit. For a high energy greyhound, you might not be able to do this much at first, but the ultimate goal is for the greyhound to have only slight tension on the leash between her neck and your hand. Think about it: you can't tie your shoe with a greyhound pulling on the leash. This is asking for real self-control for the greyhound. And once you begin to use your voice increasingly less and your physical cues become more subtle, people will be amazed at how in tune you and your greyhound are. They would not know how easy this is, and that anyone can do it.

You notice I suggest you slightly lean back and make 2 or 3 short tugs on the leash. You need to slightly lean back _so that you are pulling from your back, shoulder, and upper arm_ and not from your hand, wrist, or lower arm. You hand, wrist and lower arm are very weak and flimsy compared to the size and strength of your greyhound, and your back, shoulder and upper arm are more firmly grounded. Slightly leaning back and keeping your elbow at your side feels more defined and clear to your greyhound than an outstretched arm. Also, the 2 or 3 short tugs are the equivalent of someone tapping you on the shoulder. They say "hello, I need your attention, we are going to do something different here." This is preferable to you saying your greyhound's name 3 times, for example, which in the long run only makes her tired of hearing it. More importantly, the slight tugs increase both your and your greyhound's capacity and skill for silent communication. Besides your greyhound actually learning about the STOP cue, two other things are going on here that will be very important and useful in the future:

- your greyhound's sense of self-control is improved

- your silent communication with your greyhound is increased

Again, lengthening the amount of time you expect your greyhound to stand still can be built on from here. You can choose the length of time it takes you to tie your shoe as the immediate goal or the amount of time it takes for the traffic light to change. Work your way up to it. If your greyhound is terrible at waiting for the traffic light, take her on an alternate route for a few days until you get the STOP cue well integrated into her. The first few weeks you practice it, do it several times while out on every walk. You might even provide a treat as a reward, though not all the time. Of course, you need to develop a key word for walking on again: I simply use **let's GO** and a higher, cheerful tone of voice, but you might want to use something else.

The OVER cue
This is a very handy little cue, and if your greyhound gets it well integrated into her system, she might even do it reflexively if she gets loose, and in that way it could easily save her life. Very handy to teach a greyhound if you are out leash walking with more than one dog, pushing a pram or otherwise have your hands full. It simply signals your greyhound that you want to get to the side of the road and either stand still or move on carefully and slowly.

This is useful when you need to step aside on a narrow road for a large passing truck or tractor, on a footpath when you want to make way for perhaps someone in a wheelchair, or in any situation where you sense some level of danger and want to get out of the way.

You can just start practicing it on your regular walks by deciding several steps ahead of time just where you actually want to step aside or move over. Then, a step or two before that spot, shorten up the leash and bring your greyhound closer to your side, saying whatever cue word you choose (I just say "over"). At that point you can guide your greyhound to the side of the road and stop, perhaps even leaning your lower leg against her so she can feel that *you also are over and stopped or walking slowly with her*. Of course she can see you have done it, but letting her *feel* that you have done it too just reinforces the cue and the action that goes with it. If you have completely stopped, then wait 20 seconds and move on, using the cue word for moving on. It's worth adding that *it's different than STOP because it might not involve stopping and standing*, and because stopping is not the main idea here anyway: **moving over** *to the side of the road or walkway* is the action we are concerned with.

If you practice this on every single walk, maybe 3 times per walk, and sometimes change just how far you actually step off the road, it will pay off sooner or later. Some people in Ireland and the United Kingdom train their dogs to step off the road and lie down when a vehicle is passing. This can become so ingrained that I have seen some collies out loose doing this reflexively when a car passed, even though they might have no one with them. No doubt it saved their lives.

No more Iditerod
First, pulling like a sled dog is a common problem among all types of dogs, and for which there are many books, magazine articles, and internet postings for dealing with it. Here, I will briefly review it in ways that I

have dealt with it and in ways that apply particularly to greyhounds and similar dogs: after all, the more general advice you read about might work well for a King Charles Cavalier, but could have limited applicability for a greyhound. That said, many greyhounds are very good on the leash, but there are still many who seem to enjoy playing Siberian Husky and pulling you around to where ever they want to go. Although on one hand you might think you make a pretty amusing image to other people watching you being dragged around, it's not funny at all, and could lead to a major problem sooner or later.

Greyhounds generally are larger dogs, and have particularly strong shoulders and chests: *they are too big and too strong to not be trained to walk well on a leash.* With a properly fitted martingale and a 180cm (6 ft) leash, there's no reason why you can't take your greyhound for a leisurely walk, rather than your greyhound taking you for a drag. How successful you are at changing this depends partly on how badly your greyhound pulls and how persistent you choose to be. I could have added "how skilled you are", *but the reality is that the more persistent you are, the more skilled you become*.

A word here about prey drive, since some people tend to forgive their hounds pulling due to the common understanding – or **mis**understanding - that all greyhounds and sighthounds have an inbuilt drive to chase and kill anything small that moves. There are two main points to make here about it. First, not all sighthounds have the mythological bloodthirsty, "red haze" bouts of insanity called prey drive. In fact, many don't, and those who are fixated on killing are likely to have been blooded. This means that they received some degree of encouragement or training to do so, possibly when they were young, and almost always with very small or young animals.

The second point about prey drive is that if all greyhounds had it, then this does not explain why there are so many unwanted greyhounds every year. The excuse commonly offered for discarding a greyhound is that the hound "won't chase". Your greyhound might indeed become very excited at the sight of a small fluffy dog, *BUT it might not be prey drive*….it might be that your greyhound has never seen a dog like this before, and is wildly excited. It is up to you to decide how to handle the situation. Someone holding the smaller dog in their arms, above your greyhound's eye level, and being able to be quick IF your greyhound leaps at it, would be helpful. The bottom line is that even a greyhound with genuine prey drive can be taught how to control herself to some extent.

When you first start out walking, many dogs will be enthusiastic and pull a bit, and that's understandable because they are happy and excited. The problem is that if they are still strongly pulling after the first 5 or 10 minutes, that's not acceptable. You also might be unwittingly inviting your greyhound to pull by how you hold the leash and how you hold yourself. _If you walk your greyhound with your arm outstretched and slightly leaning forward, for example, you are begging your greyhound to pull._

In that position, you are relying entirely on your arm to control the entire greyhound. Think about it: one entire greyhound body with four strong legs, and you are attempting to control that entire greyhound with one human arm.

A person who weighs about 150 lbs/68 kg would have an arm that weighs about 8lbs/3.6kg. An average greyhound weighs about 61lbs/28 kg. So how might a 3.6 kg arm effect any control over a 28kg greyhound? And not only does your arm weigh a lot less than your greyhound, but it is a lot less agile than your greyhound too. And when your arm is outstretched, it almost exists on its own, and is not as rooted to your body than when you are in a slightly different position. _You have no leverage and your greyhound can feel this._

A few paragraphs back, in explaining how to execute a STOP, I mentioned you need "to slightly lean back" and "shorten up the leash and firmly stand still and tall, shoulders square and not looking down at her." The reason for this is because that position, with your elbows at your sides, shifts your centre of balance and automatically gives you more leverage. This means that when you do pull lightly on the leash, _you are pulling from your back and shoulder, and not from just your one arm._ The moment your elbow moves out in front of you and you also slightly lean forward, _it compels most dogs to pull_.

If you are walking in this better position, then as you start out your walk and your greyhound begins to pull, then <u>begin</u> to engage in a STOP: "shorten up the leash and firmly stand still and tall, shoulders square and not looking down at her." However, *don't stand still*, but just half-stop or pause and immediately turn around and begin to walk the other way. This will momentarily break the physical action of pulling and momentarily distract your dog. And because when you turn the other way, you are likely to be heading back for home — just moments after starting out on the walk — your greyhound is less likely to be pulling anyway, since she actually was very much wanting to go out for a walk.

As she begins to walk on but pulling less, then try to slightly shorten up the leash and gently but quickly turn and begin to walk away from home again. Her first several steps might be fine, and then she might begin to pull again. *That's fine; that's a good start.* As you proceed on your walk, you need to decide for yourself at what degree or amount of pulling you need to turn around and walk the other way a few steps...or even many steps. You might think that if you turned around every time your greyhound began to pull, you would never get anywhere, which is understandable. *You should decide for yourself what amount of pulling you will tolerate before you turn around.* For example, when first working on this, a strong but steady pulling might be acceptable for some part of the walk, but you might decide that when she begins to really lean into her harness or collar and pull with her head down and her shoulders low — as if she is pulling a heavy load — *then* you will turn around.

Once she has improved at this level, then you can back it up a little more, and turn around, for example, when her pulling causes a certain amount of tension on the leash, or when the pulling is accompanied by an increased pace. *You decide.* You can even try the STOP cue sometimes instead of turning around, and see if that helps her to recollect herself to start over. If you are consistent, then after about ten or so outings, your greyhound will probably begin (just *begin*) to anticipate you turning around every time she begins to pull, *and these are first steps towards her monitoring herself. This is the beginning of your greyhound exercising real self-control.*

Here is also where you need to remind yourself this is *just a training period*, and not what to expect for the rest of your greyhound's life. Improvement comes in stages and cannot be predicted, but the work you put in now, whether it takes 6 weeks or 6 months, is going to impact on your greyhound for the rest of her life. Keep in mind that, similar to the STOP cue, the goal is to have anywhere from slight tension to no tension on the leash.

For the New Owner or Greyhound in Training
No matter if you are new to owning a dog of any kind or just new to your recently adopted greyhound, you need to start walking her right away. This has to be done whether your greyhound is perfect on a leash or not, and whether you have been made aware of all her fears and other issues at not. You will sometimes have to make split-second judgements in these initial weeks and even months as you and your greyhound get to know each other.

For example, although you might have been told she is great in traffic, she might not ever have had a fire engine or ambulance screaming past and within a few strides of her. In such a case, you will need to decide — as you watch the screaming fire engine approaching — if you are going to just continue as if all is well, proceed with great reassurances, or avoid it all together and duck into a doorway or rush down another street. For such circumstances, it's handy to think of approaching possible threats in terms of how you might react: *proceed as normal?; proceed with caution and reassurance?; avoid?.*

As you are walking your greyhound down a familiar street, you might see ahead there is unexpected work taking place on the pavement, maybe with a jackhammer and several men in helmets and carrying heavy tools. Well ahead of time, you can think to yourself "ok, I have three options: I can swiftly pass by or slightly go around these workers OR cross the street and reassure OR just avoid it completely and turn around and go another way." You might, for example, try the STOP cue as you approach, and see how your greyhound reacts, and this can help you decide what to do. Just knowing that there are three options can often be very reassuring to yourself, and will help you make the best decision.

A Little Bit about Recall
Poor off-leash recall is one of the most common complaints about greyhounds, and for that reason I dedicated a 17-page chapter to it in my earlier book, *Understanding Greyhounds*. There is even pre-recall training that is offered in the previous chapter in that book. However, it will not be discussed that fully here, though some useful guidelines and comments are

offered in Chapter 8.

One part of the basic training of any dog that can serve as a prelude to being off leash is name recognition and basic recall around the house and garden. If your greyhound can't do THAT, then she shouldn't be off leash in an unenclosed area.

The difference between name recognition and basic recall is that name recognition is simply saying the greyhound's name and she knows you mean HER. However, no command or cue follows it. If your greyhound is maybe sniffing around the garden or eating her food or resting comfortably on the sofa and you say her name, you should see her cock her ear, thump her tail, make eye contact, or otherwise acknowledge that she heard you. It's like saying "yesssss, that's me!" She can easily learn her name by you always saying it in different ways when you are petting or massaging her or giving her a treat. In that way she learns to have a very positive association with her name.

Once she has learned name recognition, then you can start teaching her recall in and around the house. There are dozens of ways to do this, and almost all of them involve saying her name first, and then issuing a command or cue, such as "**Ruby, come here**" or "**Ruby, drop it**" or "**Ruby, NO!**". I have developed my own ideas about this, which are featured in my **Understanding Greyhounds** book, and they integrate or coordinate with some of my thoughts on off leash recall. The most important thing to remember is that *the better and most consistent you are with your greyhound at the lower levels of recall, the more this will have a positive impact when you begin off leash recall*.

Walking two or more dogs
Sometimes you might be out and about, and see someone walking more than one dog. It looks so effortless and natural: how do they do it?

Chances are it did not start off looking effortless and natural unless their walker has been doing this for a very long time. If you have two dogs to walk, you can think of the one who is easiest to walk as the "lead" dog and the less skilled one as the "following" dog. A dog who is considered easy to walk has the following characteristics:

1) tends to walk a regular pace;
2) tends to walk in a straight line unless stopping to sniff things;
3) has little to no pull on the leash;
4) stays at or near your side, not trying to cross in front or in back of you;
5) corresponds with your own pace.

Your lead dog can be given a bit more leash than the other dog, who is on the other side of you. This second dog can be thought of as the "following" dog. By giving your lead dog a bit more leash, this means she is a little bit out in front, and the following dog can see her, and she is the model for him to unconsciously follow.[7] The following dog's leash is the same length as the lead dog's leash, but just wound in your hand a few times. _If you start out by walking at a good strong pace, there is less opportunity for meandering, for crossing in front or in back of you_. As the walking proceeds, you can slow the pace a bit, but speed up again if the following dog begins to wander. Eventually you will have both dogs walking nicely, with some little reminder lessons now and then. Easy peasy.

Ah but what if there is a third dog? And a fourth? And more? The same basic principle applies: choose one dog as your lead dog for each hand, giving her a slightly longer leash - and then have the lesser dogs on either side of the lead dog, their leashes held slightly shorter, and start out at a strong, straight pace. In the photo to the right, the lead dogs are on the edges and in the middle, with the others sandwiched between them. It's worth noting here that the walker is standing tall and with squared shoulders, elbows at sides, is only about 5'3" or 162 cm, and yet has 7 greyhounds in hand.

---

[7] There are extensions you can purchase which connect the two dogs to the same leash, but for larger dogs, this has its limitations.

Tips for more than 3 dogs: it can often be a bit messy starting out, so set yourself up beforehand as much as possible. *Start off with all leashes slightly shortened, and strongly walk forward and get a decent pace going* before you begin to give more leash to them. If the walking begins to get disorganized, simply shorten up the leashes again and walk forward strongly until the dogs have pulled themselves together; then you can begin to slightly lengthen the leashes, one by one. Toileting stops can be kept organised by simply using the STOP cue.

One step at a time
In this chapter, six basic training ideas have been offered for you to begin to work on. This is just a beginning, and there are other things you can do to improve your relationship with your greyhound, too, but working on these six is a good start. You can work on them *in the order you need to,* and move as quickly or slowly as your greyhound needs. With the right equipment and these basic skills mastered, it looks like you might be ready to start visiting dog parks or places where other owners and their dogs congregate, too.

6 OUT AND ABOUT IN PUBLIC SPACES

"My greyhounds love nature as much as I do. Within the city I seek out parks and lakefront land. My older greyhound can't walk very far, but he truly loves a change of scenery so sometimes I lay down a blanket and we stretch out for a few hours. The dogs LOVE a picnic in the park in the sunshine. They are relaxed by the breezes, grass, trees, flowers and birds; they are also mentally stimulated by the presence of other dogs and people." (Dawn P, Chicago; owner of 2 greyhounds)

Being out and about is great for you and your greyhound. Aside from the benefits of exercise, it aids the bond between human and canine, builds confidence in your greyhound and makes her more well-rounded and socialized, and promotes greyhounds as pets. Your greyhound becoming confident, more well-rounded and more socialized leads to her eventually becoming a "go-anywhere, do-anything" sort of dog, and having a dog like that is such a blessing and a convenience, it's so worth it to work towards that. It won't come all at once or in a matter of weeks, but your greyhound can slowly ebb in that direction, and you won't even notice it at first. <u>If you work on it, however, the greyhound you have now is not the same greyhound you will have a year from now.</u>

This chapter is about public spaces in general, enclosed parks and dog parks, and cafés which welcome dogs. Because greyhounds tend to be larger than a lot of popular pet dogs, it's important to maintain some awareness of this, both in terms of their size on the street as people approach them, and also in terms of people who might be fearful of large dogs. So this is about the normal, expected turn of events in these places as well as actions you can take and actions you can avoid in order to prevent problems when you have a greyhound or similar dog. Keep in mind that this chapter is written with the assumption that you have a greyhound with no particularly huge behaviour problems or fears, and that you are not encountering unusual challenges on your walks or visits. It is in the next chapter that these challenges are covered. So let's get started covering being out in public in general.

There are a range of typical situations you will encounter when you are out in public with your greyhound and which are inescapable. Let's list them first and then address them one at a time.

- cleaning up poo (including messy poo)
- strangers petting your greyhound
- elderly and special needs people / small children
- other unleashed dogs
- eating food from ground / drinking from rivers and streams
- dog parks, dog cafés
- traffic issues and fear of traffic – when to reassure and when to ride through it

Let's talk about poo *(really)*
Cleaning up poo is basic and it has to be done. Always have poo bags with you. There are little poo bag dispensers which are small and lightweight and can be clipped on to the handle of your leash. Get one, and always have it filled and attached to the leash. If you don't do this, Murphy's Law is going to have a lot of fun with you. You know Murphy's Law:

Anything that can go wrong, will.

Just watch. Murphy can't wait for slip-ups for people with dogs.

You think, "*What* is she talking about? *This is a no-brainer. I'll just keep the poo bags in my coat pockets. No problem.*"

Yes, there will be a problem: one day, you will have reason to use a different coat, and, true to Murphy's Law, that is the day your greyhound uncharacteristically will have two or three huge poos in particularly public and embarrassing places…and the messiest one will probably be the most public one with the most people watching….probably under a sign about cleaning up after your dog. When this happens, the local dog warden might be watching too. People will think you are terrible, and some might even shout at you. This is just about the time you will recall telling yourself *"I'll remember to bring some with me as I'm leaving the house."* So to avoid this, it might make life easier to just get the little poo bag dispenser that clips to the leash.

Getting the poo into the bag is easy, especially if the poos are nice and firm and fairly dryish. You simply put the empty bag over your free hand, bend down and pick up the poo with the bag-covered hand, and the pull the edge of the bag back over your hand and tie the bag. Easy-peasy most of the time.

Sometimes your greyhound might have a somewhat overly soft or runny poo. No problem. You can put a layer of grass over it, especially dried grass if possible, and lightly tamp it down with your foot. Wait a minute, and try to get it into the bag the same way you would be normal poo. Sand, fine gravel, dried leaves, dirt or compost can be helpful too, as can that old rumpled up tissue in your pocket. Any combination of these is fine. If there is some residue left over that can't be picked up, then find a way to cover it with any of the above. One person I know told me she always carries a few baby-wipes with her for messy clean-ups.

 As for what to do with the bag or bags, some places will have bins for it, some will not. So yes, you might have to find a way to carry it with you. Just great. However, if you have a good supply of poo bags with you, you can line or pack one with grass and put the filled bag inside it. It might make you feel less squeamish and is protection against the bag leaking. You will quickly develop action hero superpowers for being able to detect the nearest suitable bins.

Strangers petting your greyhound
Some people really like our greyhounds' sleek bodies and elegant bearing. Many children are drawn to larger dogs and elderly people sometimes like to give them a pat in memory of a dog they once had long ago, and also because they don't have to bend down SO far to pet them. As long as your

greyhound isn't terribly fearful of people, then it could be useful to treat these requests as an opportunity to let your greyhound be a good ambassador. This doesn't mean you have to act like a high pressure salesperson all the time, but you never know what good you might do by just stopping for a few moments and letting someone pet your greyhound. Even if the person petting your greyhound is unlikely to get one for themselves, you never know who they know who might be thinking about it, or if someone passing by is impressed and it leaves an imprint on them.

The best way to let someone pet your greyhound — especially if your greyhound is relatively new to you and a bit shy — is to position yourself at one side of your greyhound, between the shoulder and the nose, and let the person stroke the other side of your greyhound, along the shoulder and back. If your greyhound seems ok with this, then let the person stroke from the top of the head to the shoulders in nice long strokes if possible. This is a good way to begin in case the person does not have a steady hand – such as a small child, someone with a disability, or perhaps someone quite elderly – and so the child is not touching your greyhound in a sensitive area, such as around the head and eyes.

After that, if your greyhound wants to turn her head towards the person who is petting, that's usually just fine. By that point, your greyhound has sensed the person's touch through her own thin greyhound skin and has an idea of what to expect next. _Doing it this way consistently "sets up" your_

greyhound for meeting people in the future and seeing it as a positive event. If you carry dog treats in your pocket, you might ask the person if he or she might like to offer your greyhound a treat. As long as your greyhound is polite with taking treats, this is a good idea, as children, for example, delight in this. And last, if you have a greyhound who is a bit shy about new people, starting out like this should help, since you are on one side of her, standing very close, not having her face them and thus possibly feel threatened, and perhaps laying a reassuring hand on her too.

Elderly and special needs people and small children
This is worth a mention because, for many dogs, some elderly and special needs people as well as children can at times be perceived as a threat or at least some unknown factor. If you think about it from any dog's point of view, someone walking with a Zimmer frame or having an unsteady gait or running towards your greyhound happily shouting or shrieking and maybe even wildly waving a toy can be intimidating. How you handle this partly depends on if you have a few spare minutes or not, because these are always situations where you need to be patient with the person and patient with your greyhound. You can't rush through it.

If, for example, an elderly person is approaching you with a walking or Zimmer frame, glance at your greyhound to note how she is reacting to it. If her ears are very alert and she is beginning to act fearful, then shorten up that leash and bring her close to you and keep moving forward. When you do this, the message you are sending your greyhound is *"We keep walking here, but I will keep you close to me."* The person approaching might even ask if he or she might be allowed to pet your dog. That's fine, just make sure you line up your greyhound alongside the person, and not face-to-face, as described above. Giving that little bit of time could make a positive difference in that person's day, and it makes your greyhound a better dog, too, and a good ambassador.

Some people with special needs might move about in a wheelchair, or can indeed be self-ambulatory. If they have some walking difficulties, or depending on the nature of their condition, they might otherwise move or talk (or both) in a way that is somewhat disjointed. In such cases where the person wants to stroke your greyhound, it always can help of there is somewhere nearby to let them sit down and gently let you guide their hand along your greyhound's back. Even if there is nowhere to sit, always make sure you are very close to your greyhound as described above, so that she feels your steady presence and is reassured.

With children, it can be difficult to gauge what is acceptable to allow and not allow. It depends on the child, and it is here you need to use your own judgement to either take a protective posture with your greyhound and let the child stroke your greyhound's back, or simply move along and save your greyhound from being stressed or feeling threatened. Keep in mind that how you deal with a 4 year old child is not the same as you would deal with a 9 year old child, which is also different than how you would handle a 14 year old teenager. Likewise, how you handle your silly, wiggly 12 month old greyhound in these circumstances is going to be different than how you handle your quiet, steady 12 year old greyhound, isn't it? The more you get to know your greyhound, the better you will know what to do as incidents continue to arise. It's also worth remembering that some children can be instinctively excellent with animals, and you would do well to encourage them. After all, some of them are just younger versions of yourself.

Other dogs, leashed and unleashed
Surely an entire chapter can be written about this, but it might be more useful to just provide some basic guidelines. Here, we are only talking about non-problematic dogs. Dealing with problem dogs are covered in the next chapter. You can also think of this as good manners that will help prevent problems, too. *Taking preventive action is always far better than correcting problems.*

When you are out walking your greyhound you will of course see other people walking their own dogs. Most of the time, you see them well in advance and can make an educated guess about how you want to continue on. Remember that some smaller dogs can be somewhat intimidated by a greyhound, others can over-compensate and become very reactive, and then of course there are the well socialized dogs who have learned to read body language. If the dog seems well relaxed and under control on the leash as dog and owner approach you, that's great, and you can just glide on by. If the owner is someone you might know and wants to stop and chat, and your dogs have never met, then standing there as they sniff each other up and down might or might not be a good idea. It does not take much for one dog or the other to get "too personal" and unwittingly provoke a small growl. This could offend the other dog, and it could all escalate quickly, and a bite is not unlikely.

Rather, if someone wants to chat, *then suggest you continue walking with them* to do so.

Why?

Because once you are moving forward, your greyhound knows what to do, knows what the rules or boundaries are, knows you are steering things, and the other dog knows this too. Here, as the two of you humans are walking forward, the dogs can give each other a quick, side-by-side cursory sniff, and get to know each other less intensively. After 10 minutes you might allow them to give each other a good sniff, and then keep walking. This is not to say that if you don't do this, that there will be a full scale dog fight! However, it IS to say that meeting a new dog this way is a lot less confrontational, and makes a potentially explosive situation less likely. It also makes a meeting between two quiet dogs even better than it might have been. *Doing it this way hurts no one, and in fact always helps a potentially bad situation to turn out well, and helps a good situation to turn into a great one.*

As for unleashed dogs, whether they are with their owner or not, it is simply best to avoid them, even if they seem friendly. *A leashed dog meeting with an unleashed dog is an unbalanced event, is not a level playing field.* They are not meeting on comparable terms: if the unleashed dog wants to playfully interact with your own leashed greyhound, your greyhound cannot really reciprocate, not in the same way and not as fully as the other dog. It's unfair, and it's frustrating, and if you allow it, then you are also encouraging the unleashed dog to continue to approach leashed dogs. If the unleashed dog is too friendly or extroverted for your greyhound, this can also lead to your greyhound eventually disliking being around unleashed dogs when she is leashed, and could be the start of a kind of fear-based aggressive reaction to being approached by any unleashed dogs.

Eating and drinking while out *(not you, but your hound)*
People throw away all sorts of leftover fast food, and when you are out in

public you would hardly notice it if you did not have a dog. Not only is your greyhound closer to the ground than you, but dogs in general can pick up a scent from very far away. It is well known they have olfactory sensors in their noses that far exceed those of humans: we have about 5-6 million sensors, and dogs have about 220 million. This means their sense of smell is at least 35-40 times greater than ours, and that they can pick up the scent of something even if it is diluted to 1 or 2 parts per trillion. So yes, no wonder when you are out walking if your greyhound suddenly begins to pull you towards a small bit of paper that seems to have nothing on it or only has a small scrap of food in it…they picked up the scent of it a good ways back! However, it's just not a good idea to let them pick up discarded food in general, as you don't really know what's in it or how long it's been there. However, if your greyhound does pick something up, don't feel that you have to run screaming to the nearest vet, but it is good to keep an eye on your greyhound for the next 12-24 hours just in case something nasty was in there.

So it's quite annoying, isn't it? You feed your greyhound twice a day and she's not starving and there she goes yanking the leash at the first scent of food out there on the ground. There are two things you can do about this:

> *1)* **_don't_** *take your greyhound out walking on a completely empty stomach; if it's just before a meal, then give her a handful of something to eat first, even if it's yogurt on a piece of bread;*

> *2) get your greyhound in the habit of not reacting* **so much** *to food on the ground. If she begins to pull you to it, you might then walk a little stronger and a little faster, holding the leash more firmly; this sends out the signal "***no, we don't do that anymore. When you smell food, we keep walking.***" After 5 or 10 times, your greyhound will understand this.*

Drinking water from puddles, streams, ponds and rivers is a bit different. All dogs can get warm when out on a walk, and might want to drink. You might think you can avoid this if you simply carry a water container and a small bowl with you, but the reality of that is water weighs a lot and carrying it and a bowl can be inconvenient. Moreover, most dogs can wait until they get home to drink water anyway. And to a dog, lapping up water that's "out there" naturally is simply fun. Free-running or flowing water is generally safe enough to drink; in a public place, if that water has been found to be unsafe, signs generally are posted. Drinking stagnant water or water from puddles are more likely to perhaps carry an algae, fungus, or bacteria that won't agree with your dog, though puddles created immediately after a lot of rain are generally not a problem.

Dog Parks!
Dog parks come in all shapes and sizes, and they can be a bit challenging to handle, no matter how happy and well-adjusted the dogs in that photo from the town's Parks Department might seem. Some dog parks are large and well laid-out, with special areas set aside for certain size dogs, and other dog parks are begrudging concessions granted to dog owners who complained a lot before the dog park materialized. Dogs parks are almost always well enclosed and have specific rules to adhere to.

The last thing you should do is bring your greyhound to the dog park and just let her off the lead right away. Instead, get to know that park a bit and visit it several times, just walking through it and as part of a longer walk. At first, it might be wise to let your first several visits take place at a time of day when there is less likely to be other dogs there who are off leash. In fact, it's possible you will encounter someone else training their new dog, and you could proceed together. As you let your greyhound get used to the sights and sounds of it, you might clip on the long leash as you walk through the park to let your greyhound begin to investigate it a bit more extensively.

You can let the park slowly become a special place to your greyhound, the place where the long leash is clipped on, where more freedom is experienced, where the sights and sounds can be more closely investigated. As you get to know each park near you, and possibly those who frequent it, you will get an idea of when is the best time to arrive, when it might be wise to avoid it, and what the general atmosphere of the place is. That nice older man with the well-behaved collie who visits in the mid-mornings might be preferable to the woman with three unleashed Yorkies and two over-active children who tend to be there in the late afternoons. One park might have better amenities than another, or a nicer group of dog owners, or simply seems safer for your dog. *Of course, letting your greyhound off leash in a dog park is not something to be taken lightly, and just because a park might be fully enclosed and you are allowed to do it, that does not mean you should.* Off leash freedom is covered separately in Chapter 8.

Dog cafés and dog-friendly cafés[8]
Dog cafés sound like a wonderful idea. What could be nicer than planning a nice long walk with a friend in a large local park, and afterwards sitting down for a cuppa in the shade of some lovely outdoorsy café located inside or close to the park? The idyllic image of people sitting at various tables, chatting away the afternoon, their happy and well-exercised dogs resting quietly at their feet, all projects an image of a great way to spend a lazy summer day. Lovely.

Well, sometimes it can be not so lovely, though there is one exception to this, and I will bring it up at the end of this section.

You need to enter dog café areas with a bit of thought. You need to have an idea of what sort of atmosphere your greyhound is able to tolerate and where to draw the line. You have to be responsible for your own dog and consider her strengths and weaknesses and which location at the dog café is best and how much time will suit her. With this in mind, there are three things to consider when you go to a dog café, and I list them here and then discuss each one.

1. the layout in terms of space for the dog as well as facilities;

2. do not assume all owners with dogs are sensible and responsible;

3. maintain some sense of your own dog's mental state.

Layout and facilities
Many outdoor cafés like to cram seating close together in order to accommodate as many people as possible; this thinking does not work well for dog cafés. There needs to be space for large and small dogs to lie down and not be very close to other dogs they don't know and not to be in walkway areas. Remember that many greyhounds are very sensitive about their feet and legs. *If people will need to step over your greyhound, you are*

---

[8] By dog café I mean a place that encourages and appears to cater to people with dogs; sometimes they will have a "dogs welcome" sign and even sell various home-made dog treats, for example. A dog-friendly café is not as accommodating, but see dogs as welcome visitors as long as they behave.

sitting in the wrong place. So before you step foot within the grounds of the café, you would be wise to first look around before entering. Don't step into the middle of it all and then stand there wondering where you might sit. Look to see if there are too many dogs, any dogs that appear uneasy, anxious, loud and might upset your greyhound, and what is the general atmosphere of the café. It might be better to return at a time when the situation is more quiet and manageable.

You might also notice the place does not seem particularly spacious, that the tables are crammed together, and it's a bit noisy. However, you don't necessarily need to leave, but instead select some seating at the edge of the area. You can park your greyhound on the side of the table and chairs farthest from the centre of activity. Here, she can get the rest she deserves, *as she is more likely to de-stress and relax if other dogs and people are not stepping over her* (amazing how that works)...... In such an atmosphere, you might also want to stay on the edge even if it's not that crowded, since you have a larger dog anyway, and let the smaller Yorkies and Chihuahuas have the centre. Most importantly, it might be wise in general to park yourself and your greyhound on the edge, especially in a busy atmosphere, in case a problem arises and you need the advantage of a quick getaway. Of course, if it's logistically possible, you can always visit the café during off-peak times and keep the visits short, gradually building up to longer durations. This is especially so for puppies, oldies and greyhounds who might be shy.

Three more brief comments here about facilities: *first*, do they have access to water for visiting dogs? After a long or even short walk, some dogs will want to drink. Some sort of a large bucket or trough with fresh water would be useful. *Second*, do you have to walk up to a counter or stand in line to pay? If the place does not have people to wait on tables, it could be very difficult if you are there by yourself. And *third*, what can you do with your greyhound if you need to use the restroom? Is it big enough to bring your greyhound with you? In terms of facilities for yourself, you might find there are some places better to frequent than others when you are alone versus when you are with another person.

Sensible and responsible owners
Not everyone attending a dog café is a sensible dog owner, and they can make things bad for everyone. Some might just not be thinking and others might not care, and both are worth avoiding. Here is a small list of factors to

keep an eye out for as potential trouble:

- *small dogs constantly barking: their shrill vocalizing raises tension in the general atmosphere;*

- *people allowing their dogs to have too much freedom while on the leash, causing the dog to get tangled and the leash to trip people;*

- *medium to large dogs tethered to tables and chairs;*

- *any size dog growling: this also creates a general tension in the atmosphere;*

- *any size dog straining at the leash: if the owner cannot hold the dog and it becomes loose, there will be trouble of one kind or another;*

- *anyone with a dog on a harsh collar, a heavy chain leash, and the dog straining on the leash: these are owners who have not taken the time to properly train their dog and either do not understand or do not care how their dog is a liability in a place like a dog café;*

- *dogs who are not well socialized to other dogs, people or new places.*

Of course we can't expect everyone and their dog to be perfect, and little incidents can happen, such as over-friendly dogs jumping up on you or being a bit invasive with your own dog. However, you have to decide for yourself where your own boundaries are in terms of how you might or might not react. Indeed, the first person to react should be the person in charge of the dog café. To begin with, it should not be incumbent on YOU to police the place! All dog cafés should have some sort of sign posted with a brief guideline in it. It could post something like:

DOGS WELCOME!
But you are responsible for your dog's actions.
Excessive growling, barking and bad behaviour in general will not be tolerated.

If a problem seems to be imminent and potentially dangerous, then let the people running the café know about it. If they are unwilling or unable to say or do anything, such as asking the offending owner to leave or move further away, then you have to decide what to do for your own safety and perhaps that of others with you. You might consider approaching the person of the offending dog, <u>but never, ever with your own dog in front of you</u>. Rather, leave your greyhound with a friend or keep her well behind your back. <u>Most important: lecturing people on their choice of dog, equipment or lack of common sense is never a good option.</u> It can easily lead to arguments. You need to be a little like Gandhi and ask yourself if you want to make enemies or you want to convince.

You might get further by simply asking them if they might move their dog a bit because their dog's behaviour *"is threatening to the other owners here and making everyone nervous."* Saying it this way relieves you of being the whining and complaining *individual*; in expressing it this way, you speak for more than just your own self. Of course, you might be addressing a person who is easily offended and tells you that it's none of your business or that their dog is "just fine as he is." At that point, it is best to retreat to another area. Of course, another person or persons might jump in to support you, but you can't count on that.

It's good to keep in mind that dog cafés are not a good place to introduce new dogs to each other. It's too crowded, too much can happen, and you don't know anything about the other dog. If you want your greyhound to socialise, do it outside the café, in a more open area. Most important for you and your greyhound, however, is that if she can't settle, then **leave.** It is unfair to expose her to something she is not ready for.

And after all that, there is one general exception to all this caution: if you have been out on a group sighthound walk, even with most of the dogs never having met before, and afterwards go to a pub or café that allows dogs, don't be surprised if the sighthounds all mingle closely with each other and there is not a bad remark among them. It's a remarkable phenomenon that happens time and again. And why is that? There are a few possible reasons that work together: *1) they are all tired from the walk; 2) the walk served as a great icebreaker, and even when they were not all sniffing and getting to know each other, they were watching body language of dogs like them that they could easily read; 3) sighthounds have been circulating and going out with hounds they have never met before for many centuries, and these walks are no different.* The photo here is of a small number of people from a large September 2016 walk in Dublin. These 8 dogs had never met, and yet they were in close quarters at the pub afterwards, and all was well.

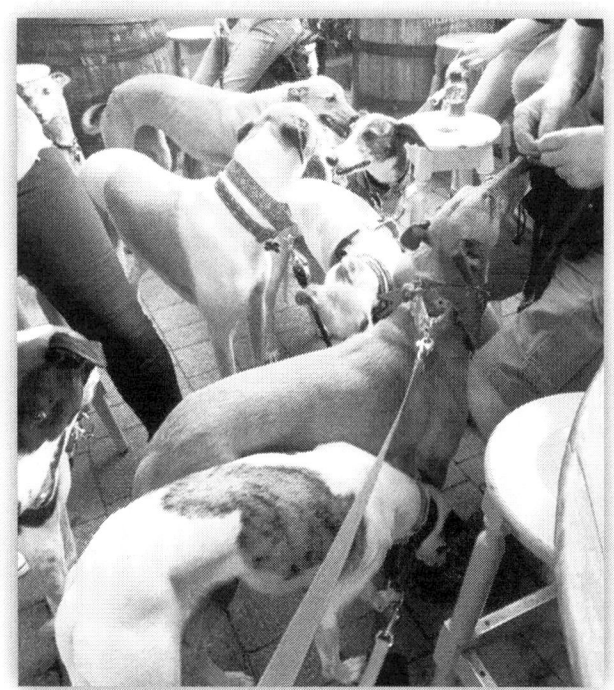

Closing comments

It's good to go out for your walks with your greyhound well prepared in all ways, and I am not just talking about having loads of poo bags! Feeling confident about how to proceed with your greyhound in questionable circumstances, knowing that there are alternatives, knowing how to prevent or avoid problems, all contribute to both of you having a great time. Going out for a daily walk, or two or three daily walks does not have to be a chore. It can be something you look forward to in terms of a break from the computer or reading, a chance to move around and stretch while waiting for food you have put in the oven, or a simple way to exercise.

Owner Marie, quoted at the beginning of Chapter 5, shows that going out walking does not always mean power walking down the sidewalk, but that it can be great for quiet moments, too:

Without a doubt, my very special shared moment with the girls in the city would be the sniffing-in-the air-moment in an empty parking lot. The girls would stop for 20 to 30 minutes sometimes, and just simply listen to the city noises and sniff the air while I would listen to music and meditate. The three of us need these moments, as simple as that, at night, in the middle of this empty parking lot. The girls started it and I joined with curiosity. After stupid or stressful days at work those peaceful stops are necessary to my own balance. No one ever noticed anything strange in the three of us just standing there. These are moments of peace during which the girls and I simply enjoy being together.

Depending on the weather, your greyhound's age and fitness and how you are feeling will always impact on your walks. For example, during glorious weather you might have one great long walk at some part of the day and one or two shorter ones, or even no shorter ones at all. Likewise during several days of rain you might choose to go out a few times for short walks. It does not have to be the same all the time. Sure your greyhound loves routine, and it is routine which builds confidence in both of you, but at some point variation in the routine can build confidence too. This in turn can lead you to be well prepared for unexpected challenges and well capable of handling them.

7 PROBLEMS IN PUBLIC SPACES & FIRST AID

"People can sometimes be their own worst enemy when it comes to repeated problems in public places. Googling can help but it can not take the place of hands-on knowledge. If you keep having a problem, speak to someone who has had practical experience and can actually show you how to get it sorted. In general, don't panic, but take a deep breath and stay calm. Having a meltdown will only make the situation worse for you and your dog." (Mary K, Dublin trainer and multiple lurcher owner)

"If any dog is suited to urban living it's the greyhound. In fact, greyhounds make wonderful pets for apartment dwellers. My tips for living with your pet greyhound in an urban environment are: when walking your greyhound be aware of your surroundings. The sooner you can spot a potential problem the more time you will have to come up with a solution. Get to know your neighbourhood. Note the streets that are more likely to have dogs or cats roaming around unsupervised. Find out where the local off leash areas are and avoid these areas if possible. Staying calm and sending your dog the right signals will help to make your walk an enjoyable one." (Sharon D, Melbourne; greyhound owner, rescue volunteer and owner of Red Hot Pet collars)

Addressing problems in public places is very important, and for that reason there are two quotes used above from two completely different people. It seems that prevention and practical experience are key, and both contributors made sure to stress how important it is to stay calm. Even though the previous chapter brought up some typical matters you are likely to encounter in public spaces, serious difficulties can happen from time to time as well. So that previous chapter must have read to be a very tame undertaking….after all, you are just simply trying to take your greyhound out for a walk. What's to know about? What can go wrong?

Perhaps it's not so much that it's a big scary place out there and something is bound to go wrong on every walk, but that now and then unexpected things can happen, and it is better that you have read a little bit about it ahead of time and then have some idea of what you might or might not do about them.

Keep in mind we have already covered in Chapter 5 that when you see a problem ahead of you – a problem of almost any kind – there are three possible responses to it:

> *1) reassuringly take a closer hold of your greyhound, letting your body language say "I'm taking over here" and just walk past it;*
>
> *2) take a reassuring hold of your greyhound, but step aside from whatever it is or make a wide berth around it;*
>
> *3) decide that the problem is more than you are prepared to handle and firmly turn and quickly walk another way.*

Of course, not every single incident can be addressed like this, but many, if not most, certainly can. Below are some common challenges:

Unleashed dogs
You don't know if the dog running towards you is just exuberantly friendly or pointedly aggressive, but no matter if it's a large or small dog, you don't like it and neither does your greyhound. Even with an owner in the distance shouting "IT'S OK, BRUNO IS FRIENDLY!!!" the fact that you have never met the owner or the dog is enough to worry you…and Bruno galloping towards you like the Hound from Hell is not comforting. You have no idea how good the owner is in assessing their dog, how long they have had it, or if there is something about you and your greyhound that has set it off for the first time.

Unless you are willing to find out if Bruno really is a friendly fellow, the best thing to do is turn and _walk_ the other way, very quickly. If you do, two things immediately happen:

> 1) if you can maneuver your greyhound to be in front of you after you have turned the other way, then your body can help to hide your greyhound from *the advancing dog's field of vision*; and

> 2) you are placing your body between yourself and the advancing dog, acting a sort of block.

If you walk away quickly, the advancing dog, with the stimulus now out of his eyesight and a human as an obstacle anyway, just might decide it's not worth it or get distracted and then retreat. If you can hear the dog still coming, you can turn your body around to face it, but with your greyhound now held in back of you. You can take one lungeing step forward and in a harsh low voice tell it to GO HOME or STOP or simply NO. Make sure you have your "leash arm" extended in back of you and that you are keeping your greyhound well behind you. Most of the time, most dogs will get this rather harsh message and back off. It would be a universal and maternal protective pose.

Even if the unleashed dog or dogs really are nice but overly friendly dogs, you have taught them a valuable lesson about not rushing people with leashed dogs. You might even convince yourself that you have just performed a kind of community service. Most importantly, the reason why you want to be able to take control of such situations is because if you don't, your greyhound is likely to start feeling apprehensive whenever any dog is approaching, even slowly, and start being reactive while on the leash, and even appearing to be aggressive. Although this point was made in the previous chapter, it is worth making here again. In this situation, it is much better for you to take control, and for your greyhound to feel that you are well able to do so.

Over-reaction of your leashed greyhound *(to almost anything)*
Dogs of all kinds can be reactive to anything, from other dogs, cats, or wildlife in their field of vision, to police officers on horseback and more. By reactive I mean over-excited, and not necessarily fearful, which generally is

a different body language. A reactive greyhound can be frightening to others because when the greyhound reacts she will sometimes stand up on her back legs, often vocalizing and sometimes vocalizing hysterically. They are straining at the leash, maybe pawing the air with their front legs, and look pretty much out of control…and they are. When they see something that stimulates them to react like this, *part of it is because they don't really know what else they might do.* That's where you come in.

Of course, it could very well be that you have recently adopted a greyhound who arrived with this problem. There is also the possibility that in the early days and weeks of living with your greyhound, you have helped maintain this problem because <u>you</u> simply didn't know what to do. One helpful thing to do is to at least begin the walk with some degree of contact with her. You can do this by leashing her, walking out the door, and stopping there or close by, then give her a treat, a quick shoulder or back massage and some voice contact too. It's a good positive way to begin a walk.

In this way, keeping your greyhound under some reasonable degree of contact with you <u>*does not have to begin when you see some problem ahead,*</u> but much further back, at the beginning of the walk. Some little reminder-stops along the way would not hurt either. You can even say it starts around the house, before you even pick up the leash, and how you are around your greyhound in general. However, at the very least, you need to start out a new walk with a fresh start, which means a type of body language and contact with the leash which tells your greyhound that you are with her and in charge of potential problems.

Part of this relates back to the body language mentioned in Chapter 5: standing tall, squaring your shoulders, slightly leaning back and with your elbows at your side, walking forward. If you start out this way, then right away your greyhound is going to feel the weight and relative strength of you, even if you are not very strong. Instead, that strength is not felt in terms of brute strength from well muscled arms, but from having increased leverage. This is especially important if you are particularly short, not very strong, or both. It means you will be starting out your walk from a position of strength and not from a position of weakness, or with a confident and in-charge body language and not a tentative uncertainty. Your greyhound will pick this up, even though you might think she doesn't notice it at all. However, after several walks like this you should see some positive shifts in your greyhound's leashed behaviour.

Until that behaviour sufficiently improves, however, you do need to react when your greyhound over-reacts. Starting out the walk as described above might help, but not immediately. So as you are out walking, let's say something takes place which makes your greyhound a bit too reactive. She stands up on her hind legs and starts barking and roaring and jumping around, completely out of control. Here you have two choices: shorten up the leash and surge forward or turn around quickly and then quickly surge the other way. Which one you do depends on what the circumstances might call for, from the degree of reaction (is she reacting just a bit, or really going crazy or somewhere in between?) to what your options are (have you just crossed a busy road and there is no way to turn back?) to your own level of confidence in yourself to handle the situation.

Regarding this last point: it might be worth telling yourself that it almost doesn't matter what your confidence level is, since you are there now in the moment and you MUST handle it, you have no choice. It might be that what to do is already laid out in front of you, and that your only option is to surge forward; that's fine, but do it, and do it well, not half-heartedly. _The advantage of surging forward is that a greyhound who is being made to move forward quickly is going to have a hard time stopping to bark, roar, and stand up on her back legs while being propelled forward._ Surging involves shortening up the leash, bringing the greyhound close to you, and moving forward very quickly, _almost at a run_.

Once you are taking control, it wouldn't hurt to have a key word or phrase to use that, in time, will signal to your greyhound that the surging is starting and that the two of you are moving forward to something else, changing the scene. In human terms, it is similar to someone changing the subject in a conversation where another person has brought up a difficult topic. Imagine a father and his difficult 16 year old son chatting with a businessman who is self-made and begins to discuss how useless education is; you can well imagine the father changing the subject and saying "George, didn't you just come back from a trip to Africa?" This is what you are doing with your greyhound: changing the subject. Your surging reaction is conveying the idea "NO, we are not dealing with THAT, but we are doing THIS."

After your greyhound has experienced you "changing the subject" for anywhere from four to ten incidents, she will begin to _anticipate_ you getting hold of her and surging or changing the subject. You can even select a word or short phrase that indicates this change. The key phrases I use are **"let's go!"** and **"we're walking!"** It can be very useful to have a key phrase or word to use at first since, as your greyhound learns it and associates it with a certain reaction from you, eventually you should _eventually_ be able to only use the words if you see something that your greyhound is about to react to. For example, as you watch that cat hiding under a car in the distance get ready to run across the road, you can use your voice _before_ the cat begins or _as_ the cat begins to dart across the road. At first, you might have to use your voice strongly, but eventually you should be able to just lightly say it. When you reach that point, some people will think you are a genius dog handler when in fact you have only put in a little extra time and thought. Don't tell them.

Over-reaction from other leashed dogs
Sometimes you might encounter another leashed dog who is terribly reactive and loves to bark and otherwise act outrageous toward any dog who dares breathe its air. This can range from a Chihuahua to a Great Dane. With such dogs, you can always simply pull your own dog closer to you and walk very briskly past the offending hooligan. If it's a particularly feisty dog who is acting this way and somehow manages to slip its collar and come barreling towards you, it is already bound to be fairly agitated or wound up. You might try quickly changing direction, but this could happen so quickly and so closely to you that there is no time to move away. There still are a few things you could try, so you still don't need to panic yet, however. Keep in mind that at this point the owner might be running towards you and screaming the dog's name repeatedly, creating more tension in the air than what you are already feeling. Depending on circumstances, you might try any of the following actions:

> 1. Take a few steps one way or another _so that the owner is also within the dog's field of vision_ and is not just a screaming voice in the background. At best, the dog could change its mind once the owner is within his field of vision; at least, even if this momentarily distracts the dog, it buys you a few seconds.

> 2. As mentioned earlier in the section on loose dogs, you can step

between your greyhound and the oncoming dog and act as a block, and then take one lunging step forward and tell it to GO HOME or simply NO. If the dog tries to negotiate around you to get to your greyhound, be persistent, be the protective mother dog, and maintain a constant position for yourself between your greyhound and the other dog. If you can slowly make your way towards a park bench, a bush, a tree, a fire hydrant or trash bin just to create even more distance between the oncoming dog and yourself, that is even better.

3. Some people carry a spray can of compressed air, which you can also use as a deterrent. You can also try squirting the dog's face with water if you carry a water bottle with you. Other possibilities are popping open an umbrella, or taking a lungeing step towards the dog and opening your coat or jacket (to make you look larger).

4. Never try to run away if there is not something immediate to run to. You cannot outrun a dog.

Extreme Fear Reaction
There might be a situation where your greyhound will have an extremely fearful and completely unexpected reaction to something. It could be anything, from a police car suddenly turning on its siren to a small child on a bicycle with noisy training wheels to the sight of something from her unfortunate past which your greyhound recognizes all too well....or does not recognize at all. When I use the term "extreme fear reaction", this is something well beyond being nervous. An extreme fear reaction can result in your greyhound becoming panicked and trying to get off the leash and run, putting all her weight into it. She might have all four feet off the ground, wrestling to get away, acting like a salmon on a fishing line, and this is because the flight response has become overpowering.

During an extreme fear reaction, it is almost impossible to bring your greyhound to your side and quickly walk away from the source of the fear. The aim is for you to stay calm and quickly bring your greyhound down _to just a slightly lower level of panic_ so that you can get through to her and re-establish contact. There are a few actions you can take, and some might work better on some greyhounds than others, depending on you, your greyhound and the situation. There is no one way to address this problem and you will have to see what works best at the time. Here are two tips:

- if it looks like the martingale or harness is about to come off, you might be able to prevent this. With a martingale, this most easily happens when the D-ring for the leash is at the back of the neck, and the leash is being pulled between the ears and the martingale is starting to slide over the ears. Immediately give a small bit of slack to the leash and at the same time move to the side of your greyhound and pull the collar back on by *pulling the martingale so that the D-ring is at the SIDE or FRONT of the neck.* You can also try to lower yourself so you are almost eye-level to the neck and then pull the martingale back away from the ears and towards the side or front of the neck. With a harness, which ever way it is starting to slip off, give it a small bit of slack and at the same time, take a step or two in the opposite direction and re-position it. This might not be the best time to try to tighten a too-loose martingale or harness, so consider positioning yourself where you can prevent the collar or harness from slipping off until you and your greyhound are in a calmer space.

- if the collar or harness are properly and fitted and so not about to slip off, then shorten up the leash so your greyhound does not have SO much room or freedom to act out. *This does not mean to make the leash very short, as severe restriction could panic your greyhound even more.* By just not allowing her to have the full length of a 6 ft/180cm lead, you can step in and place yourself between your greyhound and the source of fear, even if the fear is from a sound. *By doing so, you become more present to your greyhound and have possibly slightly muffled the sound or taken an observed frightening object out of your greyhound's line of vision.* Talk to your greyhound, touch her back and begin to move away from the source of fear. The talking and touching is to distract your greyhound's senses further away from the source of fear *and to begin to reconnect with you*. As your greyhound, perhaps still wide-eyed and panting, reconnects with you, find a quiet place to "walk it off". Briefly rub your hands onto your greyhound's face, neck and entire body, spreading your scent all over her and at the same time physically breaking up the tension that has accumulated. You have just not only reconnected but also increased her trust in you.

Fights and Attacks

Before discussing this, it's important to point out that there is something particular about greyhounds and similar dogs when it comes to fights or being attacked: <u>they have thin skin which tears easily.</u> Most sighthounds do not have layers of fat and thick coats to partially protect them. They can get injured very seriously in fights and attacks.

It is also worth understanding the difference between ***fight*** versus ***attack***. A fight would be two dogs aggressively tearing into each other, neither one showing signs of backing down, each fully engaged in fighting. An attack would be a situation where <u>one</u> of the dogs is clearly an aggressor and the other clearly a victim of that aggression. Also keep in mind there are actions that *can seem* like one or the other too. For example, a young greyhound who loves to play chase and also loves to pull the other dog down and maybe even pin the other dog to the ground without biting him is more *playing overly rough* than he is engaging in a real attack. There are also times when two dogs choose to play-fight: they make a lot of noise, play "bitey-face", maybe chase each other, but neither actually bite the other. Sometimes one might actually like to play victim and will roll over on her back and taunt the other dog to "attack" her. In these situations it could escalate if one dog gets overly excited and does not have the capacity to moderate herself, but you can prevent this easily by monitoring the rough play and making sure they back off of each other for maybe 2 or 3 minutes before they resume their rough play.

One other important distinction is having an idea of the difference between a real bite, a nip, and mouthing. To put it simply: a bite draws blood because it tears away some skin and flesh and sometimes creates a puncture; a nip involves the skin only and rarely draws blood; and mouthing or "being mouthy" means your greyhound will take your hand or wrist or whatever in his mouth but will not bite down and instead just hold you or grab you (or another dog) or pretend — in play — she is going to bite. *It's important to have a real distinction about this in your head regarding your own dog and other dogs.*

No matter if your greyhound is involved in a fight or an attack, however, the most important rule is:

NEVER grab your dog or the other dog by the collar.

You WILL be bitten, it WILL hurt a lot, and *it WILL prevent you from being able to more effectively stop the fight or attack*.

There is always a risk of you getting injured when intervening, but grabbing either dog by the collar greatly increases this.

Fights
The scenario is that you are in a public place and your greyhound agitates or is agitated by another dog and they begin to fight. This will be fast and furious and there is no point in repeatedly screaming your greyhound's name, and there will be no sense in screaming at all. **You have to resist the reflex to scream and instead, TAKE ACTION.** It's not just that it does nothing to help the situation, but that it can also do a lot to worsen the situation, to escalate tensions and intensify the raw outburst that is already in play. The aim will be to interfere with the raw outburst, to stop it, even if it's just for a moment. Why "just for a moment" ? Because in that moment you have a chance to intervene even more, which is better. Even if you somehow have been able to take hold of your greyhound's collar without being bitten, by doing so you are also restraining your dog and at the same time now making the fight so much easier for the other dog. In fact, you have just tipped the balance in favour of the other dog.

Instead, you will want to get something in between them that will affect them both. If it's possible, a bucket of cold water or even a being sprayed by a garden hose would be excellent to momentarily stop the fighting. However, that's not always possible. If you usually carry a water bottle, there probably is not a sufficient amount in it to impact on the dogs, but you can try squirting it in or towards ears and eyes. You could also insert between them anything with a long handle, such as broom or rake, and hold it between them in such a way that it interferes with one being able to effectively grab the other dog. Anything between them will help: a cardboard box, a briefcase, a piece of furniture, a coat, anything.

If you can create a momentary break and still have the leash in your hand, *simply loop it around your own dog's neck to pull her away* and then twist the two ends together. DO NOT try to clip the leash to the collar yet! Pull your dog away from the other dog and act as a block between the two of them. You can shout, kick, wave a stick, and do what ever needs to be done to deter the other dog. By this time your own dog might have composed herself and once the other dog is sufficiently far away, you can clip the leash on to her collar or harness.

In these cases, it is urgent that you act FAST *because greyhound skin can be torn very easily and immense damage can be done in the blink of an eye.*

If the other dog is much larger or is a bull breed type (such as a pit bull), then keep in mind their jaws are very strong and it will take enormous force to make them let go, and at some point your greyhound might have surrendered and now is the victim. Likewise, it might well be your greyhound who has grabbed a smaller dog and will not let go. Some say that picking up the attacking dog by their lower back legs, holding them high and pulling back will make them release, but that takes enormous courage. Recently a behaviourist who works with aggressive dogs told me about a case where a broom handle was slipped into the side of the attacking dog's mouth in order to pry it off the victim dog. This is hardly new, and was even described in 1599 by man touring England and encountering bear and bull baiting involving English Mastiffs. It was a popular enough activity where about 120 English Mastiffs were kept on hand simultaneously and a method was established for removing them from their victims: "…they did not give in, but had to be pulled off by sheer force, and their muzzles forced open with long sticks…"[9]

If you cannot find a suitable stick and there is no sign of letting up, then at worst, you might have to kick the dog with all the force you can muster, and keep kicking to make them leave, though some would say there is a risk of that dog turning on you. However, keep in mind that reporting a dog who has attacked your dog is going to get a lot less attention than reporting a dog who has attacked YOU.

Attacks
This is where one dog clearly has no interest in fighting back or defending herself, and instead just wants to get away or tries to make herself very small and instinctively takes on a defensive position. No matter if it is your

---

[9] *Thomas Platter's Travels in England, 1599* (London: J. Cape, 1937), 168-9.

greyhound who is being attacked or it is your greyhound who is attacking, you have to stop it immediately. You can use any of the suggestions mentioned above to stop it. Don't give up. Don't run away looking for help. Keep in mind that if the attacked dog is shrieking, this only encourages the attacking dog. Your intervention of any kind helps to break that up a bit.

Once you have managed to make the attacking dog stop for an instant, if possible, secure the attacked dog before it runs away to hide; this will be a purely instinctive reflex and an injured dog will even try to cross four lanes of high-speed traffic while fleeing. To secure the dog, depending on its size, you might remove your jacket and wrap it around the dog and pick it up. You might loop a noosed leash over its head and then drape your jacket or a scarf over the dog: *by draping something over the dog, you are immediately trapping body heat and possibly avoiding or delaying the dog going into shock.* To the attacking dog, who might still be there, you are placing your own scent over the attacked dog and signaling "this is MINE". If the attacking dog is your own, you need to find a way to secure him, and also be the responsible person and apologize to the attacked dog's owner and insist on paying for veterinary costs.

Sometimes you might be lucky, and the attacked dog might not have actually been injured, but was just frightened to death and screaming out of fear. If the attacking dog was not your own, and no owner seems to be nearby, *then do report it to the local police or park police, as it is so important to leave a paper trail.* If you don't report it, and the person before you never reported it, and the person after you does not report it either, then that dog would have gotten away with three attacks and no one ever having said a word about it. By reporting it, you might be preventing the next attack.

Years ago I took in a large lurcher with some bull breeding in him who, as I was to find out, had been used for fighting. He was fine within his own group of dogs but I never felt comfortable with him around other males here. A visitor who knew this absentmindedly gave him access to one of the most gentle housedogs here, and my fears became very real. The visitor tried to intervene but was completely incapable of stopping it, getting nowhere as my own dog was getting covered in bites. I stepped in and managed to make him stop, putting a small bench between him and my housedog, and pulling him away using the bench to do so. When he was about 10 feet away I could see he was still intent to return to my housedog, and I kicked him and shouted at him to go outside. It took every bit of strength I had, and the intensity of the incident is permanently burned in my mind.

If there are 2 or more dogs attacking 1 dog, the same principles apply: you need to get something between the victim and the attackers, and if you can momentarily stop the attackers — let's say with a squirt bottle shooting water into their ears — then you have created a temporary space to guard the victim. Also, if you are walking a child in a pram or a stroller, you can lift the child out and, while holding the child in one arm, shove the pram or stroller repeatedly at the attacking dog or dogs. Overall, you will need to think fast, be brave and be resourceful.

A Word about Injuries
Public places have great potential for injuries of all kinds. From broken glass to dog bites, traffic accidents to eating trash, there is no end to what a dog might get into. To discuss injuries and first aid for them would be a book in itself, and will not be covered here. However,

> ***you need to know first-aid because***
> ***it is always better to know how to stabilize an injured dog***
> ***than drive around looking for a vet.***

To give an example, it is better for the dog's sake that you know how to stop or slow down excessive bleeding than letting it bleed while you seek help. My three suggestions here are:

1) take a Saturday course in canine first aid, as it will change your life and save another;

2) buy a small booklet on canine first aid and keep it in your car or handbag or somewhere convenient, and read it now and then to remind yourself of what you might have learned in a course or to at least have some idea of what NOT to do;

3) for those times you are surfing the web for nothing in particular, go to some canine first aid sites and see if there are some recently-posted things you might learn, especially regarding greyhound first-aid.

One website you might visit and continue to check on for interesting updates is that of Dr. Lauren Pugliese in the USA. She specializes in canine first aid, and I cannot strongly enough recommend her. She does occassionally offer one-day clinics, which would be well worth attending. Here is one example of her work, showing you why a tourniquet does not have the same use for a canine as it would for a human:

http://www.activeresponsetraining.net/emergency-management-of-severe-bleeding-in-dogs

It is well worth the effort to learn some basics when it comes to emergency care.

A Safer Walk
Although some discussions here might have been frightening for some readers, at least all readers will have had some passing idea of what to do and what not to do. Maybe not everyone thinks they are courageous enough to intervene in an attack, for example, but people can surprise themselves in urgent situations. Using another example, even just knowing that you can block gives you a lot more control over a situation that you might not have otherwise had. This makes you a more confident owner, and it will be picked up on by your greyhound.

8 OFF-LEASH FREEDOM & THE RUNAWAY GREYHOUND

> *"My other dog and I just kept running after him, and I kept shouting her name as loud as I could, but she just kept funning faster and faster!"* (owner too mortified to allow his name to be used)

Poor off-leash recall is one of the most common complaints about greyhounds and similar dogs. People refer to their greyhound as stubborn, badly behaved, having selective hearing and more. The reality is this:

***off-leash recall is not a clever little trick to teach your greyhound,
and if your greyhound is not responding well,
it has more to do with you than with her.***

Off-leash recall really is more about your greyhound's relationship to you, and yours to her, than it has to do with "**obedience**". However, developing a relationship with your greyhound is rarely something that's going to happen overnight, nor in a matter of weeks. Some greyhound owners will tell you there are two levels or types of recall: one where they instinctively keep an eye on you in open countryside and are quick to follow when they see you leaving, and the other trained into them as a command. These can even be combined according to the skills and sensitivities of the owner and the hound. Most of the time it is a constant and slow-growing process.

With that in mind, there should be no hurry for you to have your greyhound off-leash in an unfenced area….maybe some day, but not at present. That's fine, however, since you are living in a highly populated area, and open spaces probably are not easily found near you anyway. For that reason, you can think more in terms of longleashing and enclosed areas, at least for now.

Because off-leash recall is such a widespread and common problem, there is a 17-page chapter dedicated to it in my earlier book, **Understanding Greyhounds**. There is even pre-recall training that is offered in the previous chapter of that same book. However, it is not going to be fully repeated here. though some basic guidelines and comments are offered. What is worth knowing for town and city dwellers is when to let your greyhound off-leash in an enclosed area, what to look for before you do, and how to react as your watch your off-leash greyhound sniffing around, and how you can prepare your greyhound for off-leash freedom in **un**enclosed spaces.

Being able to assess an enclosed area, and how you handle your greyhound's first off-leash encounters are important. So many people, for example, panic within seconds of first letting their greyhound off-leash, and begin to call their greyhound relentlessly. This is setting up your greyhound to fail, and you can compare it to letting your seven year old child loose in a toy shop and then telling her it's time to go home before she has even made it down the first aisle. Anyway, how *not* to panic and what to do instead are also among the matters covered in this chapter.

The very idea of an off-leash greyhound
Unless you have an elderly greyhound with a medical problem to slow her down, you may as well face it that you have a type of dog – a sighthound – who has been bred for centuries – for at least 2500 years – to be fast, to have an athlete's body, to delight in the great loooong stretch and pull of covering ground so fast it makes the heart pound, the lungs heave and the muscles throb. It is a lovely rush that they are born and designed to seek……even if it's only once or twice a week in a large enclosed field. If you think about what was being done with our greyhounds 500 years ago and more, they were not going out on great hunts daily, but were going out now and then. So now and then, it is very wise and it would be very appreciated by your greyhound to sometimes take her on an outing where she can feel that feeling again. As was written about greyhounds 2000 years ago by the Roman poet Gratius Faliscus, your greyhound will love the chance to *"...run more swift than thought or winged flight..."*.[10]

---

[10] Gratius Faliscus, *A poem of hunting*; Translated and illustrated by Christopher Wase (London: Printed for Charles Adams, 1654), no line or page numbering. The full quote in fact suggests a black and white greyhound as best for hunting, as follows: "Chuse the

Yes, it all sounds very romanticized, doesn't it? Many will object, starting with "But if my greyhound is allowed to run off-leash, she might..."

tear a dew claw
break a leg
break her neck
be unable to stop herself and crash
have a heart attack
somehow get out and never return
and so on.....

However, the first time you let your greyhound off-leash in an enclosed area, it does not have to be in a huge stadium and certainly not a busy dog park, but in a half acre or quarter acre field or back garden, or any public space at a time of day when there are unlikely to be other dogs. Here, in a smaller space, she on one hand has plenty of room but not so much that she would be able to work her way up to the bone-shattering speed that you fear. Here, she can improve her coordination and reflexes. If it makes you feel more confident, then let her have access to that location several times before you graduate her up to a larger space.

When she is in that space, whether it's with another dog she knows or is the only dog, as soon as you unclip the leash, it would be a good idea to look at your watch and note the time. Let her off-leash time be tracked, and decide how many minutes you will leave her loose. If you are thinking 5 or 10 minutes will do, that would be a bit unfair. About 20 minutes is more reasonable. During the first 10 minutes don't chase her or call her, but let her sniff around, maybe run if she wants. Just watch her. And wait. She might, just might, pick her head up and glance at you, and go back to sniffing. No, she wasn't dismissing you: <u>she was checking in:</u> "Right, my person is THERE, good." This is a natural reflex.

After 10 minutes, rather than calling her, move away from her, perhaps standing out of her line of vision. Wait and see if she looks up to see where you are, and whether she trots around to find you. If she does, this is <u>excellent. If she doesn't, that's fine, and it just means she is preoccupied</u>

(cont'd from previous) Greyhound py'd *(pied)* with black and white: she runs more swift than thought or winged flight."

with this new-found freedom. You might wait a bit and disappear from her line of vision a few more times, and see how long it takes before she comes looking for you. What you are doing here is re-awakening an old reflex to "stay with the pack." You are conditioning her to always keep an eye on you, something that no doubt was conditioned *out* of her early in her life. This would be the case to one degree or another for many greyhounds; it's very common.

So while she is off-leash for the first time, allow her to enjoy the time, and make sure you don't incessantly call her. You can stay within sight and sometimes step out of her line of sight. If she does come looking for you, give her a little treat or a good stroking, and then let her do as she wants. Most of all, be self-aware of your own anxieties and don't project them on to your greyhound. If she prefers to stay near you, that's fine. If she walks off and returns to wandering, that's fine too. Just let her enjoy it, and after the designated 20 minutes, stand near her, call her to you, and leash her. By then she is likely to be looking to you anyway. It's a good, first, off-leash experience, one that you can continue to build on.

Expanding Off-leash Time
After you have had your greyhound off-leash in the same area for several visits, you will have built-up her confidence a little bit. You then might want to try other enclosed areas. It would not hurt to listen to suggestions from other dog owners and also check them out for yourself. Ideally you are looking for a place that is a step up from what you have been using. The step up could be in terms of size, distractions, presence of other dogs, or anything that is not only different but makes it a bit more challenging in some way.

Your first visit there needs to be initially done with your greyhound still on the leash, and with you walking around the area completely and looking for any possible problems. These problems could range from a pond with fowl in it *(just begging to be chased)*, a stream that leads outside the park as it flows under a pedestrian bridge, a lot of broken glass, a marshy area, and more. If all looks well, you might longleash her around once or twice, and then let her off the leash. As you continue to proceed just as carefully with every new place you visit and with every new challenge you expose her to, you are also slowly preparing her for being off-leash in unenclosed areas.

Off-leash in the Dog Park
You need to be careful in dog parks. Sometimes there are unsocialised and even aggressive dogs allowed off-leash there, as mentioned earlier. Sometimes there can be very nice dogs present too, but too many off-leash can make it a bit chaotic, especially if they have formed a temporary pack. You almost have to go on a few exploratory missions and check out when might be the best time of day to go to which parks at which times with your greyhound.

Getting to know a few different parks, for example, would make it well worth figuring out that Park A is always overloaded with loose dogs and distracted owners on Sunday afternoons, while Park B is a ghost town at that time. Ok, you might have a need to go to Park A on a Saturday afternoon, but simply accept that your greyhound will only be longleashed, and that no dog should be put in an impossible situation, no matter how many other people are also doing it. Play it safe. Things can get very ugly very quickly.
Below are some basic guidelines about off-leash freedom.

<u>Off-leash and Recall Guidelines</u>

1) off-leash recall is a privilege your greyhound needs to be slowly led up to and thought through carefully;

2) if in doubt, keep your greyhound on the leash, and **never** *take chances with your greyhound being let off-leash when you are unsure;*

3) never overface your greyhound with a situation where she is likely to fail; another way to put this is to say: **set up your greyhound to succeed and don't set up your greyhound to fail***;*

4) work with your greyhound's capabilities, and not against them;

5) off-leash recall will always need some reminder training;

6) there are different levels of off-leash recall, so don't expect your greyhound to be 100% reliable in all cirumstances all the time; instead, remember what level of recall has been reached;

7) begin your recall training at home, in the house, in one room and slowly increase the level of demand or difficulty, from being in the same room to being in the next room, and then from being in the next room to being on a different floor or outside; first, make sure your greyhound genuinely recognizes her name;

8) work on recall training on the long leash when out walking, and again slowly increase the level of demand. Start with your greyhound already approaching you anyway, then try calling her with a treat reward, and then call her when there is light distraction and so on.

9) recall and off-leash problems are **_always_** the fault of the owner and **_never_** the fault of the greyhound.

The Loose or Lost Greyhound
If your greyhound ever becomes unintentionally loose or becomes lost, it can almost seem surreal. It can happen to anyone and it can happen to the most responsible owner as well as those who might not be paying attention. There are certain things to do and not do once your dog gets loose, and there are various tips worth knowing if your loose greyhound becomes lost and cannot find her way home. _Getting loose and becoming lost are two different problems,_ and although they do have some similarities in how you handle it, there are also some important differences as well. Here they are covered separately.

Getting loose
There are so many scenarios under which this can happen that it would not be possible to write them all in one chapter. Here a few examples are given, and if you ever find yourself in such a situation, you will have to adapt the responses to your own immediate needs. The two basic situations regarding your greyhound getting off-leash can range from something as mundane and eventless as a broken leash clip, to your greyhound getting completely out of control while on the leash and somehow snapping it out of your hands and bolting away in pursuit of something or in fear of something.

If your greyhound has gotten off leash in such an uneventful way that she doesn't even realize it, the first two things to remind yourself is not to panic and not to call her with panic in your voice. Instead, if your greyhound has not wandered off too far, approach her from the side in a slow but confident way and then leash her up. You might even say her name once and lay a gentle hand on her back and make her feel happy to see you. These suggestions are for instances where she has not wandered terribly far from you and is not over stimulated by being off leash in a new area. This would be the easiest "retrieve" on your part.

The next least demanding "escape" would be your greyhound perhaps snapping the leash out of your hand while intently watching something, and off she goes, disappearing into some degree of undergrowth and thus out of sight. Her attention has been completely distracted away from you. In such a case, unless you have been spending a lot of time working on her recall, your efforts at calling and calling her name is only going to fall on deaf ears. You watch in horror as she flies off after another dog in the distance, or maybe a cat or a squirrel. *There is not point trying to keep up with her, or yelling and screaming after her.* Depending on whether she is heading towards or away from traffic or something else dangerous, and depending on the level of training she has had so far, you will have a few options over how to react. Let's say she has had some very basic recall training, but nothing intensive and never to the extent that it was ever put to the test like this. There are three things you might try in this situation:

1) call her name once or twice loudly and sharply, not so much with the anticipation of stopping her, but of momentarily distracting her, slowing her down, causing just a moment's hesitation;

2) if you get her attention and she actually looks in your direction, you can either hold up the leash and show her you have it and walk towards her, using your key word for taking a walk OR you can show her the leash by dangling it and then turn and begin to walk the other way quickly. In the first action, you are sort of faking her out by appealing to her passion for "walkies" and she might very well come bounding to you reflexively. If she does, make sure you welcome her with open arms and make her feel very clever indeed for coming to you! In the second action, you are appealing to her sense of staying with her own "pack" and making it look like her pack is leaving her by moving away.

3) if she does not really have much name cognition, then say nothing and quickly walk in her general direction. If possible, it might be best if she does not know you are coming until you are close. This is because if she sees you coming from a distance, she might think you are both about to go out "hunting". This means that she will constantly run ahead of you, which is something any good hunting dog with do! Rather, stay low, stay silent, and be very quick and get as close to her as possible.

Getting Away
By "getting away" I mean situations where your greyhound is no longer connected to you with a leash, and has moved off. You might see her in the far distance, and she seems to have no interest in returning to you. <u>This is very different from the greyhound out for a run in a very large area where she enjoys dashing away from you and then zooming back to you in play</u>; this is a greyhound who is engaged with you, or is mindful of you. In such cases, it's good to keep in mind that although your engaged greyhound seems to be running *too* far away, to the greyhound herself, you are only a few seconds away!

However, with the <u>*disengaged*</u> greyhound, no matter if she is on the hunt for something or is running from something that frightened her, there is no response at all to your recall, and she is beginning to get further and further away. **<u>Don't chase her!</u>** You cannot possibly catch her and she will only run further if she sees you coming. Instead, never underestimate the influence of centuries of selective breeding to stay with the pack! If she is still in sight, slow down, and depending on the surroundings, you can try one of a few things:

- with leash visibly in hand and staying in her line of vision, try walking in an arc around her so you might approach her from the direction in which she seems to be headed; if she sees you, she might think you are leaving the area and instinctively start to run towards you; as she begins to run towards you, turn your back on her and begin to walk away from her. As she catches up to you, slow down, dangle the leash and then leash her. High praise and repeating the recall cue as you leash her up, please!

- with leash visibly in hand and staying in her line of vision, walk quickly towards another area that is <u>next to</u> where she is headed; the quick movement might catch her eye and, as above, she might instinctively start to run towards you; just like above, as she begins to run towards you, turn your back on her and begin to walk away from her. As she catches up to you, slow down, dangle the leash and then leash her. High praise and repeating the recall cue as you leash her up, please!

- if other people are with you, fan out and try to herd her towards a more enclosed area, or to a corner or sheltered area, such as the back of a building with a fenced border. If you are able to corner her, it might be best to approach her from a stooped position, and not standing up tall. High praise and repeating the recall cue as you leash her up, please!

Getting Lost

Now if hours pass and you are unable to catch your greyhound, have even lost sight of her and night is approaching, at this point she is likely to revert to survival mode, which is very common. She is likely to completely shut down to you and not respond to familiar voices and be disoriented in general. When in survival mode, dogs can almost become feral. Just like a wounded animal, they generally seek shelter in the form of a place to hide that is also convenient for watching who is coming and going and is easy to quickly exit.

From such a location, they tend to hide during the day and come out at night in search of food and water. One example I recall was when several years ago one of my newly adopted greyhounds was let off-leash too soon. She quickly got spooked and disappeared. No one could find her. A group of us when on a hunt for her late at night, and there she was, walking around in her own neighbourhood, <u>but completely passing the cul-de-sac she lived on three times.</u> We also knew she was hanging out at the back of a fast food shop very late at night, too. It took another 24 hours to catch her, but she finally was caught, herded into a narrower and narrower area until we were able to loop a slip lead on to her. She was *very* hungry, and she was fed on the spot. Just the act of being fed helped to bring her back to a more normal state of mind, and she was happy to jump into the car.

Reflecting on Off-leash Freedom

Perhaps one point that has been made very clear in this chapter is that off-leash freedom is absolutely not to be taken lightly. Clearly, a lot can go wrong if you do it too soon or in the wrong place or at the wrong time of day. Although there might be times you are tempted to allow your greyhound off-leash, _don't do it if you are not certain._ The first few times you do allow it, you need to do it in a controlled environment and under certain conditions, such as in an enclosed area at the end of a long walk when the high-energy edge is already off your greyhound. You need to create a successful and positive base of experiences, one which all later off-leash experiences are based on. This does not at all mean that you must never allow your greyhound off-leash, nor is this an excuse for you to maintain an unnecessary fear of it! All you need to keep in mind is to go carefully, take a step at a time, and remember that a few extra sessions on the longleash is a LOT better than walking the streets at 2am looking for your greyhound!

9 WHETHER THE WEATHER...

***"Will you just please stop bothering the poor dogs** and let them sleep?"* (Response from Mary O, Dungarvan Rescue Kennels, after telling her how I went out to the barn at 2am in my pyjamas to check and see if the double-coated dogs were freezing...not only were they toasty warm, but they were not at all happy to see me.)

This short chapter deals with changes in weather and temperature and how to react to it on behalf of your greyhound. Neither overcoating nor undercoating your greyhound is good for her, so it's helpful to have some basic rules of thumb to apply. The first thing to keep in mind is that our hounds do have a thermal system in their body to aid them in cooling off and staying warm. It's called thermoregulation. Canine bodies are not as efficient as human bodies when it comes to cooling off and trapping body heat, although type of coat has a lot to do with it too. Even among greyhounds, some have more dense coats than others, and some colours, like black, attract heat, so there is more to consider than you might think.

When it comes to your greyhound's thermoregulation, the number one most important factor in hot AND cold weather is WATER, or hydration. You can coat your dog all you want, or on hot days keep her in the shade almost exclusively, but they are still going to need water, and lots of it. *They need water for hydration just as much in the the winter as in the summer*, and this means *no, snow does not count!* It also means that topping up a small bowl twice a day isn't going to be sufficient either. Instead, you need to have a large bowl or small bucket she can drink from at will. This hydration requirement applies to ALL dogs, *but especially so for sighthounds, because they dehydrate so easily*.

Of course your shorthaired greyhound is going to need a coat for cold weather, but what sort of coat, how cold the weather is, how long your greyhound will be outside and what her condition is all needs to be factored in. Your greyhound is surely going to need some consideration in summer heat and sun glare, too. This is discussed at greater length in **Understanding Greyhounds**, but the basics are reviewed here.

Cold Weather
Greyhounds need coats in cold weather due to their short hair, thin skin, and low body fat. Most dog supply shops do not carry greyhound coats, and you'll be pretty frustrated trying to get your greyhound into one that's cut for a Rottweiler. They need specially cut coats due to their deep rib cages and tiny waists. I have not provided a list of coat makers because greyhound outdoor coats are very easy to find on the web. Other greyhound owners can also give you some tips on who to get a good product and good service from.

Oh, and you will quickly find there is such a wide array of coats for cold weather! Some have turtlenecks, some have hoods (really), some hang well below the elbow line, and some are so very thick and padded and insulated that a greyhound can hardly move and looks like a puffball with legs. The winter coat you choose depends on two main factors: 1) how cold it can be in the winter in your region; and 2) how robust your greyhound is. A general rule of thumb for determining if they are needing to be covered is to feel their toes and ear flaps: if these areas are cold, then coat your greyhound.

If you live in a climate where winter can be extreme, then you will probably need one coat for bitter cold temperatures that are well below freezing and also one for cool days, for just above freezing. The one you choose for above freezing temperatures would be best to have a water proof or water resistant outer shell and then some thin fleece lining it. For example, think about walking your 8 year old greyhound on a windy day where it is intermittently raining and the temperature is anywhere from 1 – 4 degrees Celcius (34-43 Fahrenheit). Both of you might enjoy the fresh air but also both want to stay dry, warm and snuggly. In less cool weather, you can loosen the coat (as you might do for yourself!) and perhaps remove it part way through the walk. On some cool or very cool days, you might want to take a short but brisk walk between rain showers, for example, and so if you are going to be moving fast, depending on your greyhound's health, you might forego her coat completely since she is likely to warm up quickly from a fast-paced walk. Keep in mind you don't want to overcoat your greyhound, either, just as you would not want to wear a blizzard-strength parka on a cool, early spring day. For cool days when it is not raining, a simple "double fleece" coat is also handy to have.

Sleeping in a cool house
Again, you need to play this by ear, according to the condition of your greyhound and how cold your house gets as well as where your greyhound is expected to sleep. So if your greyhound is expected to sleep in the kitchen or utility room at night, make sure you identify where drafts might be coming from. As mentioned in Chapter 4, you can check for drafts by putting a candle on the floor and watching the flame. If there is a draft, then perfect for this room would be a plastic oval dog bed with high sides, and the side of the bed with the opening is to be turned _away_ from the draft. Make sure the bed has something for your greyhound to snuggle into, from old blankets to a folded duvet or purchased padding. Simply putting down a rubber mat or a single thin blanket is not enough.

On very cold nights, you might want to put that double fleece coat on your greyhound too. This will keep her down in bed and toasty warm. Coating your greyhound on cool or cold nights also can help a lot with avoiding middle-of-the-night toileting demands! If you have a greyhound who often gets up in the night, even in slightly cold weather, you can trying coating her then too, as this also tends to keep them down and quiet. Often people complain their dog is up at 5 or 6am, and yet does not really want or need to go outside. This could be happening because your greyhound is cold.

There are actually greyhound pyjamas you can purchase. Some of them are very basic and others even can cover the legs almost all the way to the foot. Even the pyjamas with leg are made to be easy enough to take on and off. Most greyhounds love them, but just be careful to use them only when genuinely needed, as it is important for the health of your greyhound not to have her natural thermoregulation interfered with. To determine if your greyhound needs to be covered, use the rule of thumb mentioned earlier about feeling ear flaps and toes.

Making greyhound PJs has become a cottage industry everywhere there are pet greyhounds. There are dozens of sites for each of these regions. Here I offer just a sample of a few sources you might try, but this is only the tip of the iceberg! Several of these are also on FaceBook and Etsy.

UK /Ireland / Europe

http://www.bleakhoundsdesign.co.uk/

http://www.collarsrus.co.uk/

http://www.stokerhounds.co.uk/ (made-to-measure fleece jumpers)

http://www.lilypeeps.co.uk/

Australia

http://apieceofcloth.com.au/ (non-fleece pjs)

Oboe and Piccolo:
https://www.facebook.com/groups/291204050985804/

http://www.anniescoats.org/ (not pjs exactly but pj-like fleece coats)

US and Canada

http://www.greytfulacresfashion.com/

https://www.etsy.com/shop/greytcottagedesigns

http://www.lovedhoundz.com/

Hot Weather
The two main things to keep in mind on days when the sun is glaring and the temperature is high are water and shade. Simply put, your greyhound needs to have easy access to unlimited water at all times, and this does not mean little bowls that you keep refilling. They are more likely to drink deeply and drink their fill when they see plenty of water in front of them. If your greyhound immediately drinks every last drop from a bowl you have given her, she needs more, _now_. Nothing takes the place of hydration: not air conditioning, not shade, not a wet towel on the body, nothing. Be generous when it comes to water, please.

Of course, if you are visiting a friend or are on an outing with your greyhound, some greyhounds can be very resistant to drinking at all when away from home, even if you have brought water from home. So you need to make sure your greyhound has plenty available to her before she leaves and when she returns. If you are on an all-day outing, you might bring something with you to add to the water to make her want to drink: a splash of milk, watered-down yogurt, a bit of broth from last night's roast chicken….if you are eating a sandwich that has something in it that she likes, such as ham or cheese, you can give her one or two small pieces, and then let a few more small pieces float at the top of a bucket of water.

While on an all-day outing, or anything taking place for any length of time in bright sunlight, you need to allow time for taking breaks and resting in the shade. If your greyhound is panting, that's normal and is part of thermoregulation for cooling off. If your greyhound is panting heavily and a bit unsteady or losing strength, it's definitely time to rest in the shade and make sure she is hydrated. You might even think about bringing a water bottle for yourself as well as one for your greyhound. You can squirt it into the side of her mouth, her head tilted up, if you think this is necessary…..just don't get mixed up with which bottle is for you and which one is for your greyhound…… If she is very hot, then get a towel or t-shirt or anything made of fabric, dip it in water, wring it out, and then drape it over her body as she is lying down; this will help reduce the built-up body heat. Wading in running water can be helpful too. The idea here is to avoid heatstroke! If you live in a climate where it is frequently hot and you plan to be out in the sun frequently, then do a bit of reading up on greyhounds and heatstroke. There is plenty about it on the internet.

What about rain?
Some people have the idea that if it's raining, you really don't need to walk your greyhound. And if it rains several days in a row, ah well, we can't control the weather, now can we? Living in Ireland, however, one quickly learns that if you wait to have a day without rain, you might have a long wait. In fact, there are three expressions to keep in mind within this discussion. The first is "if you don't like the weather, just wait five minutes." Yes, many a time I have looked out the window, saw the brilliant sun and blue sky, quickly leashed up several dogs…and 5 minutes into the walk have been dumped on by rain. Here, having the right gear is essential.

And this brings up the second expression, which is a Swedish expression that rhymes in Swedish but doesn't even some close to rhyming in English: *there's no bad weather, just the wrong clothes* (det finns inget dåligt väder, bara dåliga kläder). As long as it's not dumping rain and bitter cold, your greyhound can get away with no coat or just a rain slicker. I say no coat because it is their hair along the top of their back that is the thickest and so least permeable by rain. But this leads to the last expression, which some like to claim is also from Ireland: *you're not made of sugar, you won't melt.* So get out there and go for a brisk walk in the rain: splash in some puddles, breathe in that lovely cleansing air *(and when no one is looking, open you mouth and let a few drops in)*, and be on the lookout for a rainbow.

And what's the best part of going out for a walk in the rain? Well, according to you it will be sitting down to a nice cup of tea or glass of wine, but to your greyhound??? Ahhhhh, it's the g-l-o-r-i-o-u-s sensation of being vigorously toweled off, ears to tail, and all the way down to the toes and even in between them. Of course you will be less vigorous in sensitive areas, but along the back, top of head, neck, chest, shoulder and thighs, a good robust toweling is SO enjoyed and so bonding for you and your greyhound. It is similar to the mother dog washing down her pups, in fact. Your greyhound might even start to LIKE going out in the rain just to come home to the towel-off! You can leave a towel or two in your kitchen, and as the tea kettle is boiling and then the tea is steeping...or this wine is breathing...this is a great time to start the toweling process. Your wet greyhound will adore you for it, and will look forward to the next time and the time after that!

10 A FEW FINAL WORDS

The preceding chapters were meant to cover some of the more common problems to having a greyhound in a town or city environment, but not every single issue can be covered. For example, some of the problems you might encounter would not be specific to just greyhounds, and for solutions to these problems you can consult with other owners, websites, social media, trainers, and behaviourists. Addressing separation anxiety or jumping up, for example, is not just a greyhound problem, and the demands of having a greyhound puppy are fairly common to all puppies. Hopefully the preceding chapters will give you enough information to help life in the city flow a bit more smoothly. What you need to know in more detail might be worth looking for in **Understanding Greyhounds**. In there you will find discussions on selecting a greyhound, what to do the first day and week you have brought your new greyhound home, having more than one greyhound, and many other matters.

Perhaps the most important thing to keep in mind about your greyhound is that she is from a breed type from more than two thousand years ago. This is historically accurate, as we can see images of these dogs on many ancient artefacts from that time and even before then. As time went on, these dogs were increasingly selectively bred, and became closer to a being a breed as we understand the word breed today.

They were not only selectively bred to be lightning-fast hunters, but also to stay with the pack, to be social with other types of dogs who were also used for hunting, and to be biddable to the huntsman's horn or his *halloa* (his way of calling to the dogs). Those who did not meet these criteria were not useful for hunting, were real liabilities, and most likely were culled. Six hundred years ago, for example, there was no need for any hound who strayed from the pack, ignored the huntsman's horn, and killed the neighbour's livestock.

Those dogs who have come down to us today through the centuries are the ones who had all the good qualities. Even if you have a half-greyhound, or another type of sighthound, they have these qualities in them too, and it is up to you, as the owner, carer and companion of your sighthound, to bring out these fine qualities. Sometimes these qualities are right below the surface, and emerge with ease, but some dogs have a thick layer of abuse, neglect or institutionalization that take time and care to get through to.

So don't forget that under those thin or thick layers, there is beautiful dog in there who needs to run and play a bit, splash in a stream, and otherwise indulge in the fun of being alive and loved!

They loved it then,

(from the 14th century "jewel of Welsh manuscripts" The Laws of Hywel Dda)

and they still love it today!

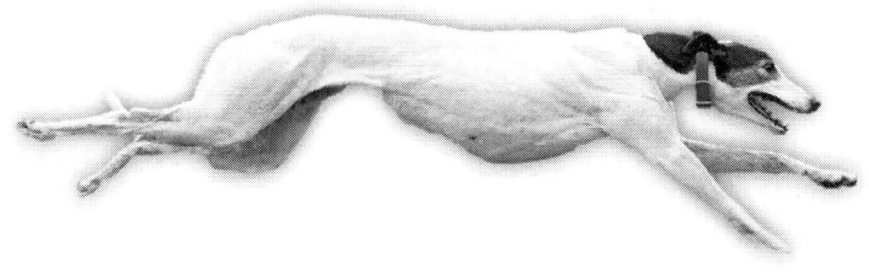

Appendix

Below are some general documents I used to hand out to adopters over the years. Now and then they were updated or edited, and these are the last versions I handed out.

****

Calming Tips
for hyper, nervous, fearful or traumatized greyhounds

There are a range of simple and low-cost to no-cost things you can do for a greyhound who is hyper, nervous, fearful, or even traumatized. <u>There is no one magic thing you can do</u>, but you will find that some things work better for you than others, and usually it is a combination of things that work the best. It is up to you to find the best combination.

Tip 1:
First and foremost is if you feed your dog dry dog food (nuts). If you do, check the bag and see if the protein% is more than 20%. If it is, then the protein your greyhound gets via the dry dog food needs to be cut down immediately. Too much protein in the dry dog food OFTEN can make dogs very edgy and irritable and anxious. **Protein directly from meat or fish is fine**; it is the *processed protein in dry dog food OR the preservatives used for the high protein* that seems to be the culprit. If you have a greyhound who has been on high protein dry dog food for a very long time, then it could be that the dog has picked up bad habits and perceptions while on it, and has maintained them even if the high protein levels are no longer being fed.

Keep in mind that even 1% too much protein in dry dog food CAN make a huge difference in behaviour<u>**. Trying to get through to a dog on high protein is like trying to talk to a drunk.**</u> I can't stress this enough. If the protein is too high, *no amount of anything else will help much*. If you have inadvertently been feeding your greyhound high protein dry dog food, STOP IT TODAY. Just cook up a giant pot of plain rice and make the next meal half the normal amount of dry dog food, and the missing half to be replaced by the rice. If you don't have rice on hand, use pasta. If you don't have pasta, use potatoes. Eventually you will find a dry dog food that is a lower protein, and you can slowly switch over to that.

Someone at the pet food shop or even a vet might tell you no studies have been done to prove this_. **_Most vets are not trained in canine nutrition._** They rely on the dog food companies to provide information. Most vets would know nothing at all about protein levels, etc. However, common sense tells you that if racing greyhounds are being fed 28% protein, and your greyhound is not currently in racing training, there is no need to feed your greyhound as if it is an athlete. If you are not going to lower your greyhound's dry dog food protein level, then don't bother doing any of the other tips listed below.

Tip 2

No matter if you have a newly adopted greyhound who is nervous or one you have had for a while like that, try this for about a week or ten days: leave out a small bucket (not bowl) of drinking water, 24/7 if possible, with several droppers of Rescue Remedy (€10 for the large liquid - don't bother with the spray!) in it. As the days pass, put a little less in it every day. This will begin to relax your dog in a general way and put him or her in a frame of mind that is conducive to learning, to taking things in and processing them rather than going in a panic or flight mode. If your dog always goes into a panic or flight mode while encountering something new or different, then he or she is not in a good frame of mind for figuring out that there is nothing to fear.

Tip 3

At Lidl they sell a type of tinned soup called Scotch Broth. It has a very relaxing effect on most dogs. Heat it up and mix half the tin into the dry dog food twice a day for 4 or 5 days, *then for the evening meal only after that*. Barley is in the Scotch Broth and it has a high satiety index, which means it feels gratifying to the dog beyond the point of satisfaction. It is also very calming because it has high levels of tryptophan, which makes you feel relaxed and sleepy. If it is real Scotch Broth and has lamb in it too (sometimes Lidl changes soup companies), then the combination of barley and lamb is a very potent source of tryptophan. When ever I get in a really nervous or anxious dog here, I get Scotch Broth. Sometimes I just get it anyway, if, for example, the dogs here are beginning to pick a new habit that winds them up too much. You can read all about the qualities of trytophan on the web.

Tip 4

Before your greyhound goes to sleep at night, pour a bit of boiling water into a small bowl with maybe 2 tablespoons of porridge oats in it - let it sit for a few minutes, then mix in a drop of milk and give it to your greyhound - it has a quieting affect on the dog so that he or she sleeps through the night, awakens well rested, and has had the benefits of the oats on the central nervous system.

Tip 5

You can also mix the above oat mixture directly into the dry dog food (yes with the barley) - it has inositol and B-vitamins in it, which are excellent for the central nervous system. The dogs here get it daily – also excellent for immune system as well as skin and hair.

Tip 6

If at all possible, get your greyhound tired every day for the next week or two through ball chasing, running in a large enclosed area, going for long fast walks, etc. Again, this is not for the rest of your greyhound's life, just for the next week or two. It will get him or her into **_a pattern_** of exercising and then resting, then getting up, eating those relaxing foods, etc. It will act as stress relief, will allow your greyhound to sleep deeply and well, and will also create confidence.

Tip 7

Massage your greyhound! It does not have to be a long session. Start at the head between the ears and with 2 or 3 fingers together, begin to press down and make massaging circles on each vertebrae. Even in the places where you can't feel the vertebrae, do it anyway, and do it all the way down to the tail and back up again. This is very bonding and your dog will love it. Massage the legs, too, starting at the top, working your way down to the toes, and massage each toe firmly. *This can be very helpful in gradually, very gradually working towards being able to cut the nails of greyhounds with sensitive toes.* Massage the tail, from base to tip, and gently with your hand about 4 or 5 inches from the base, give it a slight pull to the left, then to the right and do it again. Make sure you gently massage your greyhound's flanks, the soft stretchy fold of skin at the top of the thigh and after the ribs. They LOVE this. I call it "the mommy spot". This is the most bonding place on a dog, and I am told it is where the mother dog's sniff them to identify their puppies. Any dog newly arrived to me gets a nice massage there. Massage the ears, the ribs, anywhere. This is all very bonding and confidence building. Massage should be firm but gentle: push, but not too hard.

Tip 8

Get down on the ground with your dog, at eye level, and play with him or her. You can play-bow, bark, whine, roll on to your back, pant, bat him with your "front paw". This is also very confidence-building. Many dogs will initially be in shock or startled: they have never seen a human do this. Consider that you have suddenly been placed in a home in Mongolia, and after three weeks someone speaks English to you. That's the same response your dog will have. The first few times in fact your dog might get really silly, as they get delighted that you are "speaking dog" with them.

You can determine which things seem to work best on your dog. It might be that some things work better for some family members, and other things work better for other family members. All the suggestions above will contribute towards creating new patterns and habits of being a pet greyhound after a week or so. He or she will always feel full, relaxed, calm, well exercised, etc. If you embark on this right away, you should begin to see some positive changes in about 4 or 5 days, though some people report they see changes much more quickly. _The whole point of this is to get a relaxed greyhound, because a relaxed greyhound can learn about the world around him or her, and a nervous greyhound can't._ You can gradually start doing less of the more demanding things, but do keep up with the low-protein etc.

Two More Tips

1) before you go out, put a coat on your greyhound. If it is a coat with a thick fleece lining, it will feel warm and comforting and she/he might be less likely to get up and walk around and "make trouble" if she/he is feeling warm and cozy, especially after a nice walk! This also is a trick I use to housetrain dogs at night.

2) put some of your **unwashed** pillow cases or t-shirts in the dog bed or or, if you don't use a plastic dogbed, then with the bedding. We forget how important scent is to our dogs, and your scent in the sleeping area will be

reassuring. If possible, create more than one sleeping area in the house.

After about 4 days of any combination of the above tips, you should definitely see improvement. I would be surprised if you didn't.

****

FEEDING TIPS
and things you can add to food to encourage a healthy coat and skin

dry dog food or dog nuts - no more than 20% protein should be given to pet greyhounds! The higher the protein, the more you are making your greyhound a *racing* greyhound. The extra protein CAN go to their heads and make them edgy and nervous. Look for dog food that indicates it is "good for digestion", as this usually means it does not encourage runny poo, which is impossible to clean up in the garden! <u>Here, in the morning the dogs have dog nuts with some sunflower oil or yogurt mixed in during the day or sometimes just plain. They eat about half a liter of dry dog food in the morning and another half liter at night. At night they get a hot meal of dry dog food (nuts) mixed with something meaty or fishy, a heaping handful of uncooked oats, and hot water. This is all mixed up to make a sort of stew, and it settles them down for the rest of the night and gets them ready for sleep.</u>

2 or 3 teaspoons of oat (porridge) flakes mixed in with the hot meal, daily - this is rich in niacin and thiamine, which is excellent for healthy skin and hair growth - all my dogs get it daily. It also has inositol in it, which strengthens and relaxes the central nervous system.

sardines in sunflower oil, one sardine every other day - this is high in the Omega oils and Vitamin A, the latter being excellent for healthy skin and hair. You can mix this in with the hot meal, or give it separately as a treat. Too much Vitamin A is toxic, so one sardine every other day is plenty.

sunflower oil - a teaspoon or two of this in the evening meal on the non-sardine days

cider vinegar - once or twice a week, on a warmish sunny day, just before going out for a walk, here is something good for a greyhound's skin and hair growth, and good for bonding: in a small bucket or basin just mix a solution of half very warm water and half cider vinegar. Dip a cloth into it, partially wring it out, and go over the entire body with it, stem to stern, and let it soak down to the skin. DON'T rinse it off. Take the dog out for a walk in the sunshine and the vinegar scent will dissipate. The vinegar changes the ph balance of the skin and creates an inhospitable environment for any sort of parasite. It also leaves the coat and skin smelling fresh and clean, and puts a shine on the coat. I am also convinced it creates optimum conditions for rapid hair growth around wounds.

one more thought - when you mix meat/fish into the dry dog food, shred the pieces so they are very small. In this way, the dog is not having to absorb and process large chunks of rich food, which makes digestion easier and more efficient, and could help any loose poo problems the dog might be having as well. The smaller pieces also make a better "gravy" when you add hot water to the dry food and shredded meat.

****

For first-time greyhound owners....

...no matter if this is the first time you have owned a dog at all, or the first time you have owned a greyhound, there are a few things you need to know about them and how they might differ from other types of dogs you have experienced.

First, greyhounds are part of a larger group of dogs called sighthounds, just like an Airedale and a Jack Russell are part of the larger group called terriers. Sighthounds are dogs which hunt by sight and scent, and it is a type of dog which is literally thousands of years old. You can find images of lop-eared and pointed-eared sighthounds on ancient Egyptian artifacts as well as artwork from ancient Greece and Rome. This means that these dogs have been around humankind for a very long time, and so have become sensitized enough to read us well. Although over time the basic small-waisted, deep chested sighthound has evolved into separate breeds such as the saluki, the Afghan Hound, the Scottish Deerhound, the Irish Wolfhound, the Sloughi, the Pharoah Hound and others, the greyhound as we know it today first became recorded about 1000 years ago, when certain laws in England were developed in regard to the control and ownership of these prized dogs. Generally all the sighthound breeds were highly prized, and either were only owned by nobility or were treated as a member of the family. In North Africa, for example, there is the expression "it is not a *dog*, it is a ***sloughi***", showing that they believe these dogs are separate, apart, and better than the average *dog*. Wolfhounds and deerhounds are very common in early Irish and Scottish history and myths, and greyhounds were often very favourably referred to in very early English literature. Well-socialized sighthounds often "recognize" each other when out walking, and read each other's body language very well - for that reason it is very easy to mix the different sighthound breeds.

In Ireland, greyhounds have come to have a poor reputation, and are not seen as suitable pets, even though tens of thousands of greyhounds are adopted as pets throughout the world every year. People in Ireland assume they are cross and nervous, but in fact a truly cross greyhound is hard to find, and a nervous one is often the product of poor ownership. In order to promote informed and responsible ownership of your new pet greyhound(s), here are some basic points you need to know about your new family member(s):

- do NOT feed your dog a dry dog food that is more than 18-20% protein. Often, but not always, the extra protein can "go to their heads", and they can become nervous, jumpy, and even irritable.

- many Irish veterinarians *are not accustomed* to treating pet greyhounds, and do not realize they MUST have a completely different anesthesia. If they are administered the incorrect anesthesia, they will die, and in fact several rescued greyhounds have died when brought in for neutering to inexperienced veterinarians. Some vets might not even believe that greyhounds need a different anesthesia, but information about this is very easily found on the internet. If you want to find a good vet experienced with sighthounds, then ask others who have pet sighthounds or your adoption place.

- many greyhounds are sensitive to raised voices, threatening arm gestures, and brooms and mops, as they have often been treated with impatience and rough handling. Please be gentle but firm with your greyhound.

- all dogs love routine - it makes their lives predictable, and this makes them confident and calm. Do establish a very clear routine for them, especially when you first get up in the morning and before you go to bed at night.

- the first 4 or 5 days are the most difficult for your new greyhound(s). Expect there to be some whining or anxiousness. Taking the new dog in and out for several short walks can be very calming and reassuring, as the walking out and coming back establishes for them that THIS is home, this is the place they go back to every time.

- when people come to visit, don't have them put their face directly in the dog's face when first meeting (how would YOU like it?). A few gentle strokes on the back, shoulder, down the throat, etc, is much better for the dog, less confrontational and not at all confusing.

- if your greyhound gets loose, call your dog to get its attention, but don't expect it to run up to you immediately. Instead, call the dog's name a few times, and turn and walk a few steps the other way - sighthounds almost always want to follow their people and stay with the pack, and knowing to do this can help out in many emergencies. Of course, in a situation where there is a lot of traffic, you will have to do your best to slow down the traffic and also try to somehow corner your dog if it is too frightened.

- most people feel greyhounds are large dogs, and are easily frightened by them if they are running loose, and even if they are leashed. Promote greyhounds as pets by encouraging people to stroke your dog, and don't let your dogs off-leash if there are other people around who might be frightened, especially children.

- greyhounds have thin skin and many boney prominences - always make sure your greyhound has somewhere soft and padded to rest and sleep on. Otherwise, they develop pressure sores very easily.

- greyhounds lose body heat VERY quickly and so need to wear coats in cold weather as well as in cool and wet weather. If they are constantly cold, their systems will use the calories from food to stay warm rather than stay in good weight, and they will lose weight very rapidly. Try to always keep your greyhound in good weight, and make sure it is wearing a coat outside in cold weather.

- your greyhound craves human companionship....after all, they have had it for many centuries! Make sure your dog gets lots of positive attention but is not allowed to torment you for it! Grooming and damp-cloth rub-downs are a great way to keep your dog clean and also bond the relationship. More than anything, they want to be with YOU, their special person or special family who looks after them and gives them a reason to be happy!!!

****

HOUSETRAINING TIPS

It would not be completely unusual for there to be some toileting accidents during the first week or two as your new dog adjusts to the the new home environment. The best defence is to take her out frequently and give her high praise when she "performs" outside, and use an unhappy tone when an accident in the house does happen. Also take note of the time of day it tends to happen and where it happens. For example, if the dog is getting up to pee at 4 or 5am, then take away access to water after maybe 6pm. If the dog is peeing near the door, then that means your dog wants to go out and has been perhaps a bit too subtle in giving you a hint or you have not noticed how the dog is signaling you. Some dogs, for example, just will start walking around and will not settle, and it might seem at first that they are just being a bit restless for no reason.

To be prepared for an accident in the house, the best way to deal with it is to have ready some old towels and a mixture of Flash or some other highly scented cleaning fluid. I use a scolding tone as I splash the cleaning fluid right on top of the pee and throw a towel over it, pouring a bit more cleaning fluid and letting the dog hear my disapproving tone. This is what I do for all dogs arriving here with no housetraining, and it works great. The thinking behind doing it this way is that by splashing the cleaning fluid on top of the pee, in the dog's mind you are "peeing" on top of its pee, which in dog language is showing you are having the last word, being somewhat dominant. In addition, the smell of the scented cleaners might be nice to us, but dogs HATE it. It will make a dog disinclined to pee in the same place. And a scolding tone as you clean up - *"what dog did this? who did this? what a naughty dog!"* and so on will stand in stark contrast to the high praise the dog gets outside.

However, please NEVER hit the dog. They won't quite make the connection and in case you have adopted a dog with a sad past, it will just make them fearful of you.

ABOUT THE AUTHOR

Mary Fox has been living with sighthounds for much of her adult life. Besides running Orchard Greyhound Sanctuary for more than ten years, she has worked to promote them as pets and introduce welfare legislation for them in Ireland. Mary is also the author of **Understanding Greyhounds: Our Companions Through the Ages**. She lives in County Offaly, Ireland.

Printed in Great Britain
by Amazon